MW01033293

BEYOND COLLISIONS:

How to build your entrepreneurial infrastructure

Cover illustration: Ayleen Bashir

Interior design: Point Graphics

Printed in the United States of America.

ISBN-10: 0692999892
ISBN-13: 978-0692999899

First Edition

DEDICATION

To our husbands, Mark and Tony, and our supportive families. And to everyone who contributed to this book: you are the future of economic development.

Contents

ACKNOWLEDGEMENTS

This book owes a great deal to the many entrepreneurship support professionals who so generously shared their thinking, their expertise and their stories with us. Without them this would have been a very short paper!

Joe	Ballegeer
Ayleen	Bashir
Christi	Bell
Patricia	Blakely
Jim	Brasunas
Lauren	Caldwell
Steve	Case
Duamed	Colón-Carrión
Peter	deSilva
Stephanie	Devane
Brad	Feld
Siobhan	Finn
Pola	Firestone
Mark	Galeassi
Ravi	Gangele
Linda	Ghaffari
Dell	Gines
Angela	Gonzalez
Wendy	Guillies
Tammy	Halevy
Verne	Harnish
Conaway	Haskins
Jeff	Hoffman
Mike	Hoffmeyer
Tim	Jemal
Sandy	Kemper
Norris	Krueger
Amy	Kuhlers
Penny	Lewandowski
Pam	Lewis
Robert	Litan
Michelle	Long
Tom	Lyons
Dara	Macan
John	Machacek
Deb	Markley
Steve	Massa
Mary	Maus Kosir
Kevin	McCurren
Joey	Medellin
Jennet	Miller
Erik	Monsen
Sarah	Mote
Joseph	Picken
Steve	Radley
Vanessa	Roanhorse
Denisse	Rodríguez
Gerald	Smith
Frank & Kimberlee	Spillers
Sherry	Turner
Vanessa	Wagner
Ann Marie	Wallace
Mark	Werthman
Rob	Williams
Kelly	Wilson
Kathy	Wyatt

FOREWORD

Here's the story behind entrepreneurial infrastructure.

Entrepreneurship support started at the grassroots. Government wasn't doing it, the private sector wasn't doing it. So nonprofits came into being, trying to help entrepreneurs. The support resources were fragmented because they all developed independently.

In 2010, when the Ewing Marion Kauffman Foundation published a report[1] showing that a significant number of jobs were being created by new and young firms, people got interested in supporting entrepreneurs.

When you look at traditional economic development, there are defined processes for attraction and retention of companies. There are site selection teams, data that is gathered, marketing teams – there's a whole supply chain that goes into attracting companies.

With entrepreneurship there is no infrastructure, and as much as everybody wants to keep the ephemeral, organic quality of entrepreneurship, entrepreneurs want structure. They want to know where to go and what the next point on the path is.

We really do need to build infrastructure to support our entrepreneurs. It may not look like traditional infrastructure – roads, sewers, utilities – but it will be infrastructure. We can already see some of it developing. The front end is clearly meetups, Startup Weekends, other kinds of collision events. That's become part of the infrastructure. Events like these bring people together. Network connectors like SourceLink are part of the infrastructure. And all those resources that have developed independently are part of the infrastructure. So is the capital that entrepreneurs need and access to innovations.

We are at an experimental stage in building entrepreneurial infrastructure right now. Some things will stick and some will not.

Clearly, part of the infrastructure is the connections. People want to be part of TechStars (an accelerator program) so they can be connected to the

[1] Dane Stangler. "High-Growth Firms and the Future of the American Economy." Ewing Marion Kauffman Foundation, April 7, 2010.

TechStars network. How people flow between organizations, resources, connections is becoming a central question.

We are past the organic stage. We are talking about mainstreaming entrepreneurship.

A Practitioner's Approach to Entrepreneurship

This is a story about pioneers. Many of the people you will meet in this book and the stories you will hear are from people who have been laboring in this vineyard of entrepreneurial infrastructure for decades. They've been the entrepreneurs of entrepreneurship: trying things, pivoting, making things happen. We are going to tell you stories of what they did to support entrepreneurship in communities of all sizes, how it worked, why it worked and some of the awesome results we've seen.

We want to be very clear on a few points. This is a practitioner's approach to the subject of entrepreneurial infrastructure, not a purely academic look. We have drawn heavily on our own experience in building entrepreneurial infrastructure, beginning in Kansas City and spreading to about 25 other communities, as well as the experiences of some really bright people with whom we've had the good fortune to work.

This is not a book about how to help entrepreneurs, how to grow a company, how to raise capital. There are lots of great books on those topics and if you email us we'll send you a list of our favorites. At the risk of sounding academic, consider this difference:

"Knowing how to bake a cake is clearly not the same thing as knowing how to bring together all of the ingredients for a cake. Knowing how to bake a cake is knowing how to execute the sequence of operations that are specified, more or less closely, in a cake recipe. The list of ingredients is understood to be contained in the recipe, but the recipe is not fully revealed by the list of ingredients."[2]

This book is about assembling the ingredients, not baking the cake.

You may be looking for a step-by-step guide to building the next Silicon Valley. That's easy. Build Stanford, and wait 100 years. You don't want to

[2] Sidney G. Winter (1968). Quoted in "The Changing Frontier: Rethinking Science and Innovation Policy," 2015.

build the next Silicon Valley … you want to build the best version of your community that you can. And we can't even give you a magic silver bullet for how to do that.

What we can do is share what we've learned about entrepreneurial support networks, entrepreneurs themselves and four actions that seem to work in most communities to help build the entrepreneurial infrastructure that helps entrepreneurs start, grow and succeed.

A Beginning, A Middle, An End

The book is organized in three parts. The first part answers the core questions: why should you care about entrepreneurship, what is an entrepreneurial infrastructure, who are these entrepreneurs that we want to help?

The second part gets into the nuts and bolts of what you can do, in your community, to support and encourage entrepreneurs. We've developed a roadmap to follow as you identify resources that support entrepreneurs, connect them, empower the network and measure results. Those steps are: Identify, Connect, Empower and Measure (Figure 1).

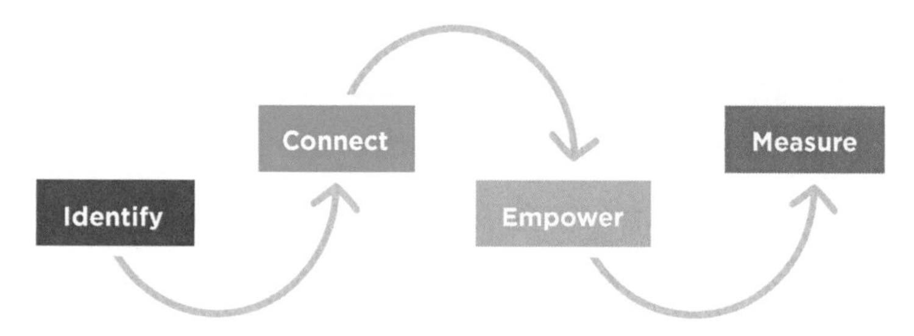

Figure 1: Steps to develop entrepreneurial infrastructure

The third part of the book talks about strategies that will help you accomplish those four steps. We've shared some insights we've gained about marketing, funding and leadership. Finally, we give you the vocabulary list we all wished we had when we started in this field, the Rosetta Stone for the alphabet soup that is entrepreneurship support.

We're going to talk a lot about Kansas City throughout this book. We believe that some of the things that have happened in the Kansas City metro area can serve as a guide for other communities. And we've seen actual results here.

This approach works in rural and urban communities, large and small … even if you don't have a mountain or access to an ocean. Start by identifying what you already have in your community to support entrepreneurs and business owners. Connect them together. Empower the resources to collaborate and fill gaps. Then measure what happens.

"Most successful entrepreneurs at some point articulate and use a business plan to guide their ventures. Communities should behave no differently. A smart game plan … is a critical piece of becoming an entrepreneurial community."

-Don Macke, Deb Markley and John Fulwider,
***Energizing Entrepreneurial Communities* 2014**

A piece of advice: start small and build. Be an entrepreneur. Try the first step and see how it goes. Engage your customers. Pivot if you need to. You don't need a big report or a 30-page plan to get started.

Just start.

If you don't take a step today, you'll be in the same place tomorrow."

-Maria Meyers, founder, SourceLink

Why This Book

Maria: My interest in entrepreneurship dates back a long time. I was at several large organizations. At various times in my career we hit tough times, and I had to lay off a number of employees. I really wanted to be in a place to help organizations create jobs and help people move seamlessly into another position when the market shifted. Entrepreneurship is a platform for doing that. Empowering people to become self-sufficient and follow their own entrepreneurial interests puts both the onus and control on them. I wanted to create … and solve problems.

I got that chance when I started KCSourceLink® in Kansas City in 2003. Working with the resource organizations, community leadership and the entrepreneurs themselves, we've developed a vibrant entrepreneurial ecosystem that actively works together to fill gaps in entrepreneurial services – and spark new economic opportunities for small business owners. The crossings and connections have established a strong framework, an infrastructure, that allows our entrepreneurial ecosystem to flourish.

I'm excited every day when I see and hear the stories of how entrepreneurship has changed individual lives and lifted the entire community.

Not long after I founded KCSourceLink, I started getting calls from across the country from people who had heard about what we were doing and wanted to do the same thing in their communities. Becoming a national consultant was completely organic. We found that while every community is different, the principles we'd applied in Kansas City worked in communities large and small, urban and rural. It's all about listening, collaborating, finding and filling gaps. We've seen some remarkable success in the Kansas City market. Our connected network of resource organizations numbers about 240.

We've made it easy for entrepreneurs of all kinds to connect with resources that help them start and grow their businesses. We've been cited by several organizations as the #1 city for business growth (Wednowver-InsightPRM Business Growth Report); #2 best city for women in tech (SmartAsset), #2 most improved metro area for startup growth (Kauffman Index of Startup Activity), and in the top six cities that offer better value for growing startups (Forbes). We've been awarded almost $15 million in federal and state grants for programs like Digital Sandbox KC, a proof-of-concept program; Whiteboard2Boardroom for technology commercialization; and ScaleUP! Kansas City for second-stage businesses. And we saw a 290 percent increase in the available capital for early-stage companies from 2013 to 2016.

I've been asked to speak many times on how to do this: how do you pull together the pieces in a community into a strong entrepreneurial infrastructure. Since I tell the same story every time, I thought maybe it was time to capture what we've learned in a format that would be easy to share.

They say it takes a village, and it really does. I've been so fortunate to work with amazing partners and community leaders in the Kansas City market and throughout the country with our SourceLink® affiliates. Thank you for sharing your energy, ideas and experiences. This book wouldn't be possible without you.

Kate: I've been encouraging Maria to write a book for at least 10 years, and I finally got her to say yes.

My involvement with entreprencurship dates back to my time at the Kauffman Foundation. I joined in 1991, when the Foundation was first exploring the idea of supporting entrepreneurs, and I had the privilege of being the first marketing director for the Center for Entrepreneurial Leadership.

I felt like I had a front row seat for the entrepreneurial revolution. I worked on some incredible programs like FastTrac®, the Kauffman Fellows Program, the Global Entrepreneurship Monitor and Global Entrepreneurship Week. And I worked with some of the brightest people in the business: Michie Slaughter (first CEO of the Kauffman Center for Entrepreneurial Leadership), Jeff Timmons (trailblazing professor of entrepreneurship at Babson College), Ray Smilor, Marilyn Kourilsky and Jana Mathews (senior leaders at the Kauffman Center for Entrepreneurial Leadership and entrepreneurship thought leaders) and so many more.

It's been great fun to work with SourceLink for the past 10 years, first as a consultant and now as an associate. Like any startup, we've had the chance to try a lot of new things, pivot when appropriate and help a lot of people in the process.

For me, the driving force has been the model of the late, great Mr. Ewing Kauffman, founder of the foundation that bears his name. In the early days, it was a bit of a challenge to convince the philanthropic world as to why a foundation would want to support entrepreneurs. Mr. K always said that the best social program was a good job … and that the more people we could help create businesses, the more jobs we'd create. He was right.

Section 1

WHY ENTREPRENEURIAL INFRASTRUCTURE MATTERS

"The concept of an entrepreneurial ecosystem refers to the collective and systemic nature of entrepreneurship. New firms emerge and grow not only because heroic, talented and visionary individuals (entrepreneurs) created them and develop them. New ventures emerge also because they are located in an environment or "ecosystem" made of private and public players which nurture and sustain them, making the action of entrepreneurs easier."

-The Financial Times Lexicon

Economic development has been all about jobs. What many economic developers don't realize is the impact entrepreneurs have on job creation in their communities.

The history of economic development has been focused on attracting large employers to a community, keeping large employers in a community and promoting real estate development. Supporting startups and small and emerging businesses has not been a high priority, for a few reasons:

- A community doesn't see an immediate benefit when you grow your own entrepreneurs; there's no headline like when a plant opens and brings 450 jobs
- Economic development organizations are typically measured on attraction of new companies and retention of existing large companies

But as Nobel Prize winner Bob Dylan observed, "the times they are a-changing," and so is economic development. It's become more and more difficult to attract large companies to a community, and they frequently stay only as long as the length of the incentives they received.[3] Entrepreneurship has joined big company attraction and retention as a

[3] Katie Mauer. "The Effectiveness of Tax Abatements," 2005. Retrieved July 2017. http://www.umich.edu/~econdev/taxabatemts/

key strategy in the economic development world for a couple of reasons

- Net new job growth can be attributed to young, growing firms[4] (Figure 2)
- Companies that "grow up" in a community are more likely to stay in that community; most companies make decisions to start and grow in a community for reasons other than economic incentives[5]

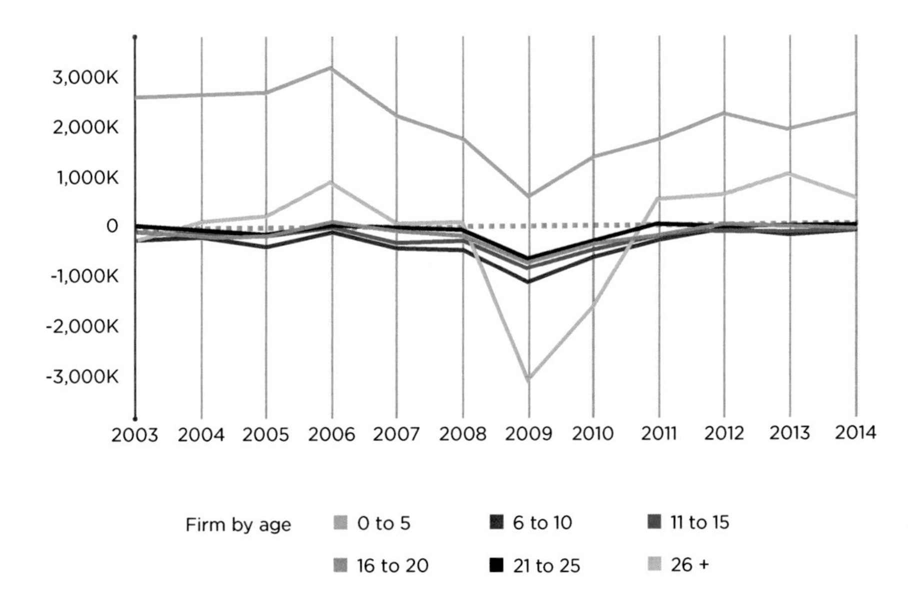

Source: U.S. Census Bureau Business Dynamic Statistics and the Ewing Marion Kauffman Foundation in 2017 State of Entrepreneurship Report.

Figure 2: New and young firms have been the net new job creators for the past 25 years

Economic developers have a critical role to play in building an entrepreneurial infrastructure. We know you can't quit your day job: attracting new companies and retaining large firms will always be part of how you measure success. This book can help you with the third part

[4] Jason Wiens and Chris Jackson. "The Importance of Young Firms for Economic Growth." Ewing Marion Kauffman Foundation, 2015.

[5] Endeavor Insight conducted surveys and interviews with 150 founders of fast-growing companies in the United States. This research, reported in What Do the Best Entrepreneurs Want in a City? (2015), found two things that founders valued above anything else: a pool of talented employees and access to customers and suppliers. The report also noted that entrepreneurs of fast-growing firms based decisions about where to live on personal connections and quality of life factors, and few cited business-friendly regulations as reasons to start a business in a specific city.

of your job (nurturing entrepreneurs) by giving you practical, tactical suggestions. We're here to guide you.

Entrepreneurship in Unexpected Places

According to Steve Case, founder of AOL, entrepreneurship is not just happening in Silicon Valley and Boston. In his book *Third Wave* he talks about the changing nature of place and entrepreneurship.

"The First Wave took place from 1985 to around 1999. It was about building infrastructure for an online world. When AOL launched, 3 percent of people were online. By the turn of the century … we had literally gotten America Online.

"The Second Wave, from 2000 through 2015, was about building on top of the internet. The Second Wave was defined as a service – social apps like Twitter, Snapchat and Instagram make sharing ideas and photos easier, or traffic apps like Waze.

"The Third Wave is the era when the internet stops belonging to internet companies. I'm convinced that the coming of the Third Wave will be closely linked to what I refer to as "the rise of the rest." In the following decades we will see cities that were previously in the margins of growth entrepreneurship rise up and become entrepreneurial powerhouses.

"Growth entrepreneurship is possible anywhere in the United States and in any industry. Third Wave entrepreneurs will be farmers, factory workers, chefs and artists and will bring innovation to industries and cities they are already in.[6]"

Growing the Pie

Building an infrastructure helps you move from helping people one at a time to creating a system that moves the entire community forward. It levels the playing field, making opportunities more visible and accessible for people from any number of backgrounds, and creates a sense of "we're in this together" rather than winners and losers.

The nice part about growing your own entrepreneurs is that it's not a zero sum game. When you are recruiting a new plant, some other community has to lose for your community to win. Michie Slaughter, the first CEO of the Kauffman Center for Entrepreneurial Leadership, encouraged communities to think about entrepreneurship as a way to move beyond just

---

[6] Steve Case in "Kauffman Index: Growth Entrepreneurship." Ewing Marion Kauffman Foundation, 2016.

getting "a piece of the pie." He encouraged the use of entrepreneurship to make the pie bigger, rather than fighting over the crumbs.

Sandy Kemper, CEO of C2FO, a successful fintech company in Kansas City, talks about this in another way, using a river vs. reservoir metaphor for wealth, with a river representing a renewing and growing set of resources while a reservoir represents finite resources.

"There is a difference in communities when people with wealth are more passive and less entrepreneurial; they tend to think of wealth as a reservoir … Everything you take out is a zero sum game. You think of what you have as being more constrained.

"In a more entrepreneurial community it's a river. Everything you take out is replenished."

Kemper noted that it's not just geographies within the United States that take these differing views about wealth and risk.

"*The vast majority in China see wealth as a river. In China, it's happening so fast, they are not thinking it's finite. In Europe, it's a small, highly guarded reservoir."*

The other interesting thing is that supporting a creative, innovative climate that encourages entrepreneurship can turn around and make it easier to attract those large companies that are looking for the "cool factor" as well as access to talent that is often attracted by a community of energy and collisions.

"These cities create a virtuous cycle in which employers are attracted by the large pool of potential employees and workers are drawn by the abundance of potential employers … In highly entrepreneurial industries, workers get ahead by hopping from firm to firm … An abundance of local employers also provides implicit insurance against the failure of any particular start-up."

-Edward Glaeser, *The Triumph of the City* 2011

An Environment for Entrepreneurs

Mark Werthmann, an economic development representative with the U.S. Department of Commerce, has seen many changes during his 25 years in the economic development field.

"Economic development has seen a number of transitions over the last few decades. At one

time, it was all about recruiting large, new businesses and industry, usually from another state or city. Then business incubators became a big trend because communities began to understand that growing small businesses was an important part of an overall economic development strategy. Business incubators filled a need for small businesses to have a place to start, have access to services and get established before they went out on their own.

"Business recruitment and retention are still important components of economic development and business incubators still can fill a need. As the economy and technology have changed, communities have recognized that their economic development program has to have the ability to adapt and change. Many communities are trying to figure out how to create a system that will attract, develop and nurture many different types of businesses. It's not necessarily about a place but creating an environment that will allow existing businesses and entrepreneurs to grow and thrive.

"It takes years to develop a successful economic development program in a community. The community has to figure out what they do best, what resources they have and what their focus should be. Most successful communities invest in these programs and create these environments over many years.

"Communities cannot expect to have great economic development results if they aren't willing to invest the time, money and focus needed to achieve these results. These investments aren't just limited to business investments. The community has to consider investments that make it a more livable city, such as transportation, schools, infrastructure and other local amenities.

"Today, communities are not just competing with the city 50 miles away but ones that are half a world away. It's a never-ending challenge for many communities. As quickly as economic, political and social changes occur, communities have to be able to adapt and change.

"There is no quick fix or silver bullet to create a successful economic environment."

Shifting the Focus to Entrepreneurship

The good news is that many in the economic development field are already shifting their focus to entrepreneurship. According to the 2016 International Economic Development Council (IEDC) survey released by IEDC director Jeff Finkle, almost 50 percent of those who responded to their survey had increased efforts in entrepreneurship. About 40 percent had altered their organization's strategy to include greater emphasis on entrepreneurship and small business development.

Why I'm interested in entrepreneurship (from the SourceLink survey)

Entrepreneurs create jobs, attract young professionals, establish vibrancy in a city and attract capital.

E-Ship infrastructure will be key to rural community survival and growth.

To build and sustain a reputable "pipeline" of investment in intellectual capital, innovation and forward-looking opportunities that keep us competitive through the 21st century.

It is important to grow such infrastructure in South Africa, where we can offer and pool holistic resources.

An entrepreneurial infrastructure leads to like-minded individuals with varying skill sets that can accomplish greater things because it is generally tied to a passion.

We are interested in entrepreneurs' ability to create jobs and diversify metro Detroit's economy, which historically has been overly reliant on a single industry.

Entrepreneurship is often described as the key to economic growth for communities. For our community, economic growth is important, but it is even more important for resolving the income equality gap. Creating opportunities for underrepresented groups is key for us in a majority-minority city.

Because if we don't the city will gradually die.

Entrepreneurs are likely the best prospect for economic growth in our rural community. So, developing the infrastructure to support them is absolutely critical.

Having a strong entrepreneurial infrastructure reflects positively on the community as a whole.

Entrepreneurs should not accidentally happen upon the resources they need to grow. We should have a predictable and deliberate process available to them to become connected to networks for growth and education.

SourceLink conducted its own survey with a number of economic development professionals and collected about 50 responses. More than 86 percent said supporting entrepreneurs was a high priority. (See sidebar for comments.)

Successful infrastructure

Almost three-fourths of the respondents said their communities had a successful entrepreneurial infrastructure. More than 50 percent called their entrepreneurial infrastructure "emerging" as opposed to dormant, established or vibrant.

Efforts to support entrepreneurs

Almost 60 percent described their communities' efforts to support entrepreneurs as proactive. Twenty-four percent characterized such efforts as reactive, and 17 percent said neither description clearly defined their communities' efforts. They said the key players in their entrepreneurial infrastructures were fairly evenly distributed, with entrepreneurs topping the list.

Obstacles facing entrepreneurs

Access to capital was cited most frequently as an obstacle facing entrepreneurs, followed by resources not visible and entrepreneurs unconnected.

Measuring an entrepreneurial infrastructure

Among those surveyed, jobs was the number one way of measuring a successful entrepreneurial infrastructure, followed by startups, collaborations and the sustainability of the support network (Figure 3).

Building an entrepreneurial community is not a quick fix. Entrepreneur and venture capitalist Brad Feld, in his book *Startup Communities*, suggests a 20-year timeline. In Kansas City, it took about 10 years to have an "overnight success," and the answer to "are we there yet?" is "no." There will be lots of victories along the way, but there will also be days of just slogging along, trying to keep the momentum moving in the right direction. Don't give up.

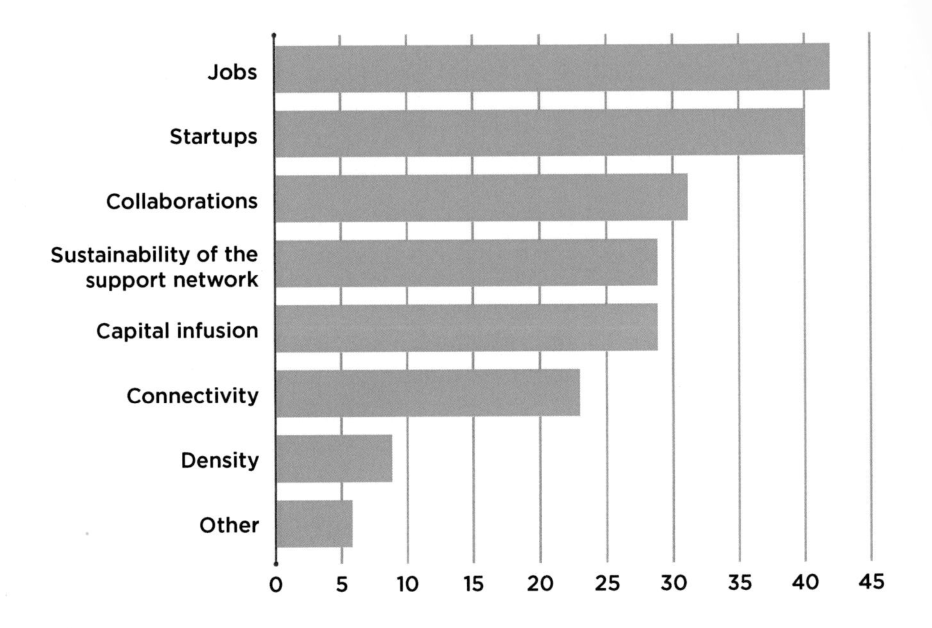

Source: SourceLink survey of economic development professionals, 2016.

Figure 3: Top measures for a successful entrepreneurial infrastructure

A key point: You can't just open an incubator or an accelerator or a coworking place and call it good. We know no one consciously thinks like that anymore, and yet we are constantly amazed at how many communities jump to a specific program solution before they really understand their community, their entrepreneurs, where they have gaps. Don't be that person. There are any number of amazing programs out there to support entrepreneurs, and we're going to talk about a bunch of them. Just don't jump into programs first. Get to know your community and what it needs. Talk to your entrepreneurs. Talk to the people who work with them. Work in the white spaces.

What's in It for Me?

Entrepreneurship and a strong entrepreneurial infrastructure matter to a number of different audiences, sometimes for different reasons.

Economic developers are beginning to recognize the role of entrepreneurs in job creation. Since most economic development organizations measure their success in terms of job creation to some extent, it is in their best interest to discover how to encourage and nurture entrepreneurs and add "creation" to the economic development mix of "attraction" and "retention."

Corporations accrue several benefits from working with entrepreneurs. First, innovative companies can be the source of new products and services for the larger corporation, a kind of outside agile and nimble R&D department. Entrepreneurial firms provide investment opportunities for corporations and an opportunity to contribute to the bottom line. Small and emerging firms can be a critical part of a large company's supply chain. And, by encouraging executives to mentor innovative firms, larger corporations can re-energize their own workforce and bring that entrepreneurial mindset and drive into their everyday strategies.

Entrepreneurial support organizations have the most vested interest in entrepreneurs. Their missions call them to be of service to these companies. They are frequently measured by how many entrepreneurs they reach and the collective impact of those companies in terms of jobs, startups, debt/equity investment and sales increases. But measuring entrepreneurship goes well beyond "jobs and starts." We'll talk about that and how to measure entrepreneurship along the continuum. Plus an interconnected network of resources allows entrepreneurial support organizations to refer clients effectively, prove their value, build their communities and lessen the amount of duplicative services.

Many **universities** have added economic development to their mission of service – and relevance – to the community. The focus on entrepreneurship is a natural step toward that mission, as it serves both current students and alumni. Universities engage in entrepreneurship from the standpoint of taking research-based innovations to market and capitalizing on the talents of their faculty, an important piece of revenue diversification. They also teach entrepreneurship: in 1985 there were 280 courses in entrepreneurship offered in U.S. colleges and universities; now more than 5,000 courses are offered along with associated extracurricular activities.[7]

Investors who are looking for a return on their investment need good deals in which to invest, just as entrepreneurs need access to pools of capital. Entrepreneurial firm development functions as a pipeline. For there to be opportunities for later stage investments, there must be many firms started. Investors have a role in encouraging the beginning of the pipeline to be filled with promising young firms. Many investors reap deep financial rewards from finding the next big innovations early and helping mentor those companies to mutually beneficial success.

[7] Dan Schwabel. "How Colleges are Becoming Entrepreneurial." July 8, 2012. Retrieved July 2017. https://techcrunch.com/2012/07/08/how-colleges-are-becoming-entrepreneurial/

Philanthropy has become more interested in entrepreneurship as the focus has shifted toward self-sustainability. More and more philanthropies want to teach people how to build the fishing rod versus handing out fish. In particular, community foundations in rural communities have become interested in entrepreneurship as a way to grow their own businesses and ensure their long-term survival. These community-based businesses create job opportunities for young people, contribute to the tax base and bolster fading downtowns.

Of course, **entrepreneurs** are interested in entrepreneurship. For the most part, they are not terribly interested in the entrepreneurial infrastructure. They just want the services they need when they need them. Like other infrastructures – transportation, communication, utilities – people just want the roads to be smooth, the radio to work, the water to run and the lights to go on. They recognize when things don't work – when resources are difficult to access, when funding is difficult to secure, when entrepreneurs leave the region for better opportunities.

That said, some entrepreneurs will get engaged in particular projects and will take the lead on organizing the community. And that's great.

Entrepreneurship lies at the crossroads of community organizing and economic development and we need all players to come together to build the infrastructure, rally the allies and tell the story.

What Happens When People Interact?

Building a strong entrepreneurial infrastructure in your community can yield tangible results. For example, it could translate into a more transparent and accessible process to creating a business, yielding more entrepreneurs in your ecosystem because barriers are removed and the process is easier. Results could also include more successful exits, improved access to capital or visible and relevant resources. Because every community is different, with different challenges and goals, results are different.

Here are a few examples of communities' results:

- Loudoun County, Virginia's network of resource partners provides assistance in marketing, financial planning, sales, loans, business planning, technical support, education, government contracts and operations. The work has paid off: over the past decade Loudoun County has seen 40,000 net new jobs created.

- Relationships formed by KCSourceLink's resource network helped propel EyeVerify (now Zoloz), a 2012 startup from the University of Missouri-Kansas City, to a 2016 sale of more than $100 million. The community, working together, has nearly quadrupled the pool of capital available to entrepreneurs to $752 million.
- NetWork Kansas's E-Community Partnership has loaned more than $9.7 million to 360+ businesses from 2008 to 2016, leveraging more than $47 million in private investment.
- Grow North, a Minnesota organization serving the agriculture and food industries, signed on more than 100 resource providers in less than two months.
- Colmena66 in Puerto Rico has recently brought together more than 150 resource providers to create a unified network to help entrepreneurs across the island.
- In its first year of operation, Baltimore SourceLink assisted 445 startups and existing business owners in the Baltimore city area.
- During Global Entrepreneurship Week 2016, IASourceLink partnered with the Iowa Rural Development Council to bring together 75 rural Iowa communities for a day of planning around entrepreneurship, growth and prosperity.

Small steps and big strides, these communities are collaborating to increase visibility to resources and access to entrepreneurial empowerment. Communities working together to build entrepreneurial infrastructures are well positioned to accelerate economic growth.

Make Entrepreneurship Easier

Denisse Rodríguez Colón, COO of Codetrotters, has experienced firsthand the need for entrepreneurship support in her native Puerto Rico.

"Since the recession started 10 years ago the population in Puerto Rico has decreased by 3,000 each month. The local market is shrinking. Businesses have to be prepared to weather the storm. Regulations to start and run a business are very difficult to navigate. The permitting process and tax regulations are difficult, even for accountants. Agencies are slow and difficult to access.

"It took four months for my sister to receive a permit to operate a food truck business. She was paying rent for four months but couldn't operate her business without the permits. We reached out to people we knew by phone and Facebook. Not everyone has those contacts. The process should be transparent. This hinders starting new businesses."

Colón left a banking career at Goldman Sachs in New York to work for change.

"I felt the need to go back to Puerto Rico and become part of its transformation."

Currently she is involved in several entrepreneurship support efforts, including CodeTrotters (an academy for coders) and Colmena66 (a network of entrepreneurial resources). These programs provide an opportunity for Colón to fulfill her aspirations to change the Puerto Rican economy for the better.

"We try to support businesses that can scale outside of the island. We ask new business owners to visualize their business outside Puerto Rico. It takes education to change their vision of their business. Exporting is not in our DNA. We are used to being able to sell locally. We are reaping results from this process. I work with a boutique that now has ecommerce. We connect businesses with the tools to help them."

The work of Colmena66 is having a profound impact on entrepreneurs in Puerto Rico.

"Thanks to Colmena66 we learned about EntePRrize, the business building competition and accelerator by Grupo Guayacán. Since the start of the program, we have grown and strengthened the base of our business. We are so grateful to Colmena66 for making the connections that boost small businesses and in turn help Puerto Rico's economic growth."

-Angela Gonzalez, founder, Feliche Artisan Yogurt
San Juan, Puerto Rico

"Colmena66 has provided our company with that crucial connection, that for years we've been looking for to establish our farm operations. Now we have the ideal scenario to grow what we always envisioned."

-Duamed Colón-Carrión, president, Agro Tropical, Inc.
San Juan, Puerto Rico

Let's get started by answering a key question: What is an entrepreneurial infrastructure?

1. WHAT IS AN ENTREPRENEURIAL INFRASTRUCTURE?

"Every individual that we can inspire, that we can guide, that we can help to start a new company, is vital to the future of our economic welfare."
-Ewing Marion Kauffman

"Regional development leaders need to recognize that ideas, talent, capital and a culture of openness and collaboration are all vital to regional startup communities, which are best thought of as innovation ecosystems involving complex interaction among entrepreneurs, investors, suppliers, universities, large existing businesses and a host of supporting actors and organizations."
-Ian Hathaway, Accelerating Growth: Startup Accelerator Programs in the United States, *Brookings Report*

Let's start by defining some terms. Before we get to what an entrepreneurial infrastructure is, we have to understand what an entrepreneurial ecosystem is, how it grows and who drives it.

If you go to any conference for economic development professionals, you'll likely find a session or two on "entrepreneurial ecosystems." An ecosystem is defined as a group of interconnected elements, formed by the interaction of a community of organisms with their environment."[8]

There are several excellent models of what makes up an entrepreneurial ecosystem. Dan Isenberg, professor of entrepreneurship practice at Babson College, and Victor Hwang, author of *The Rainforest*, have produced two of the most frequently cited models. Organizations such as the World Economic Forum, the Center for Rural Entrepreneurship and the Aspen Network of Development Entrepreneurs have all looked at what goes into a supportive environment for entrepreneurs.

Almost every model includes six key areas: Finance, Policy/Regulations, Support/Connections, Culture, Human Capital and Markets. It's worth considering these elements when you are identifying the gaps in your infrastructure.

---

[8] Dictionary.com.

The key difference between ecosystem and infrastructure is that ecosystems emerge, almost organically, from a number of different actions and activities. No one organization or person "creates" an ecosystem. We can, however, build an infrastructure that supports, encourages and sustains the elements that make up a healthy entrepreneurial ecosystem.

"You can't create entrepreneurial communities, they create themselves. You can create the conditions in which entrepreneurs choose to innovate. You can work across government and universities and private-public partnership lines to make it easier for entrepreneurs to start and grow companies."

-Peter deSilva, former head of the Greater Kansas City Chamber's Big 5 Initiative on Entrepreneurship

Brad Feld, in his book *Startup Communities*, suggests that the ecosystem has to be led by entrepreneurs, that the ecosystem is formed by what entrepreneurs do and how they connect within their communities. But he also points out that "feeders," the organizations that feed and support entrepreneurs, have a role to play. And that's where entrepreneurial infrastructure comes in to support, nourish and sustain the entrepreneurial ecosystem.

From innovation to infrastructure

Conaway Haskins III, extension specialist at Virginia Tech and leader of SourceLink Virginia, notes that the economic development world is discovering entrepreneurship, but tends to focus on programs rather than infrastructure.

"(I was) at a roundtable this summer with university entrepreneurship programs from all six inhabited continents. It didn't matter if they were in Kingston, Jamaica, Casablanca or South Korea. They were all looking at accelerators and startup weekends.

"The environment is changing and we've always got to be thinking about the next thing. When we launched (SourceLink Virginia) in 2014, it was innovative. Now in 2017 it's infrastructure. We have to be able to make that shift mentally and organizationally."

-Conaway Haskins III
SourceLink Virginia

"In a startup community, the leaders have to be entrepreneurs. Everyone else – universities, government, non-profits, investors, service providers and large companies – are feeders. Both are critically important but play different roles. In the absence of a critical mass (at least a dozen) entrepreneurs playing leadership roles, a startup community won't be able to build any long-term momentum or sustainability. The second any of the feeders try to organize or control the startup community, things will stall. Now, individual members of feeder organizations can and should play leadership roles – but this has to be done by participation at the individual level, not through the hierarchy of the feeder organization.

"For example, let's take a university entrepreneurship program. Instead of focusing all of the activity internal to the university, having speakers come through and talk to students, and assuming that the startup community will revolve around the activity of the university, I encourage a different approach. Leaders within the university (professors or deans who are interested in entrepreneurship and the head of the entrepreneurship program) should get involved with the local startup community as individuals. They should figure out programs that bring the students out to the startup community, which could include internships, lectures, site visits and meetups around specific topics. Then, the university, which often has plenty of space for larger events, can be a convener for the startup community and host things once it has developed these relationships."

Feld makes key points: entrepreneurs should be at the center of any entrepreneurial development efforts and relationships across sectors are critical to sustainability.

As people who want to support entrepreneurs and business owners, we can make it easier for entrepreneurs to make connections. Feeder organizations can use their resources to engage with entrepreneurs and contribute where it makes sense. Case in point: behind most 1 Million Cups is an organization that provides the space and buys the coffee. We can do other things that work in the background for entrepreneurs: make it easier for people starting businesses to find the right resources; simplify the process of getting permits or licenses; provide a continuum of programs to help entrepreneurs vet their ideas and grow their businesses; help bring new pools of capital to the community.

Look around your community. Really look. Your community has organizations that are doing something to help people start and grow businesses. It may be a chapter of SCORE. It may be a business development center. It may be a university program. It may be a Startup Weekend. It may be a pitch competition for the local high school. It may be a regional rural development center.

What we see in so many communities, and what we saw in Kansas City in the early 2000s when we were starting KCSourceLink, are business support programs operating in isolation. Think of those programs, those assets, as a bunch of Lego® blocks, without an assembly guide. If you start by attaching one Lego block to another, connecting one program to another in a deliberate continuum of services, you start to build something.

Connect several Lego blocks together and you've got a base. Little by little, brick by brick, you connect the dots and that support network for entrepreneurs and business owners gets stronger. Before you know it, you have a house and then an entire village, with the roads and bridges that allow entrepreneurs to travel from one place to another.

That's building an infrastructure for entrepreneurship. Not trying to order a kit so that you can build the Boston version. But taking what you've got and knitting it together so that, taken as a whole, you've got a system of interconnected parts that does make it easier for entrepreneurs to start businesses, find resources, recruit talent, attract customers and connect to capital.

You'll also have a bird's eye view of the gaps in your community. What do entrepreneurs need that is not being offered?

Throughout this book we will talk about building an entrepreneurial infrastructure, and outline specific steps that you can take in your community to begin snapping the first bricks together. We'll describe specific levers that economic developers and others interested in supporting entrepreneurship can use to make a difference in the day-to-day life of an entrepreneur.

Through almost 15 years of on-the-ground research, SourceLink has identified levers that contribute significantly to an entrepreneurial infrastructure. Just as roads and water lines and bridges are needed to support overall economic development in a community, so too do entrepreneurs and small businesses need infrastructure. Based on experience in the field actually building entrepreneurial support systems, SourceLink has developed a model, which includes:

- Resources
- Networked capital
- Pipeline of ideas
- Talent/workforce development
- Corporate engagement
- Storytelling

Resources. Entrepreneurs need connected support networks that provide trusted referrals to investors and other funders, as well as experts in operations, marketing, technology, sales and dozens of other business-related services. Fortunately, many communities have an abundance of business development resources, but often entrepreneurs can't find them or find the right one for them. With a multitude of different kinds of businesses and a multitude of resources, a central point for visibility and connection can help strengthen businesses and accelerate their growth.

Networked capital. Capital (debt, equity, grants) is the fuel that propels businesses forward. Entrepreneurs and business owners need the right funding to develop prototypes, take ideas to market, open storefronts, finance executive talent and fund expansion. Communities need networked capital and a continuum of funding to address the needs of starting and growing businesses at all stages.

Pipeline of ideas. Engaging research institutions and corporations to match ideas with seasoned entrepreneurs will give rise to new innovation and move ideas from the whiteboard to the boardroom. In many communities, the people with the passion to drive innovations into the marketplace are unconnected to the pipeline of ideas.

Talent/workforce development. Developing businesses need access to highly skilled and motivated talent pools. STEM and entrepreneurship education at all levels, from grade school to graduate school, can help create the qualified workforce of the future.

Corporate engagement. The landscape of most communities includes a range of corporations and foundations that can support entrepreneurship. Immersing these companies fully in the entrepreneurial ecosystem brings invaluable expertise, connections and resources to generate spin-outs, ignite research and help startups succeed. Linking these institutions can also leverage funding from outside of the community to fill funding, support, mentoring and other gaps by creating much needed resources.

Storytelling. Healthy entrepreneurial ecosystems share the good news. Stories of success provide hope and inspiration, encourage support of entrepreneurs and resource organizations, and help create a climate of risk taking. In most communities the story of entrepreneurship is fragmented and no one organization steps up to take the lead to define the vision, set the direction and shape the story.

What's really important is what YOUR community needs, where your community has strengths, what your entrepreneurial infrastructure looks like. Building an entrepreneurial infrastructure is less like building a model airplane, with step-by-step instructions so that the finished product looks a certain way, and more like fixing Thanksgiving dinner: you have to find out what people want, what you've got in terms of supplies and what you need, who has the competency to help in what areas. Some of the individual dishes may have a prescribed recipe, but no two Thanksgiving dinners turn out exactly alike.

Many different kinds of enterprises make up a healthy economy. Who are the entrepreneurs in your community?

2. WHO ARE YOUR ENTREPRENEURS?

"Scholars have been unable to agree on a definition of 'entrepreneur' in the 75 years or thereabouts since Schumpeter[9] produced his seminal work on entrepreneurship."

-William D. Bygrave, *Theorizing about Entrepreneurship*, 1991

What do we tell our entrepreneurs? Know your customers.

If we are going to build an entrepreneurial infrastructure to help entrepreneurs and business owners be more successful, it makes sense to know the audience. And for the purpose of this book, a common way of describing entrepreneurs will get us all on the same page.

After working in the entrepreneurship space for almost 15 years, we've seen many definitions of entrepreneur.

- Entrepreneurs = those firms with the potential for high growth
- Entrepreneurs = those in the concept and startup phase
- Entrepreneurs = those with an innovative, game-changing product or process
- Entrepreneurs = those starting or growing a technology-based company
- Entrepreneurs = those with the intent to grow a business of significant size
- Entrepreneurs = those creating their own wealth

These are all correct.

Working in communities across the country, we've found that it's helpful to cast a wide net in describing entrepreneurs and the resources that support them. We've come up with what we call the "Quadrants of Entrepreneurship" because it takes more than just one type of business to create a healthy, economically vibrant community.

[9] Joseph Schumpeter. "The Theory of Economic Development." 1912. Highlights the function of the entrepreneur.

Four Quadrants of Entrepreneurship

Innovation-Led

Innovation-led enterprises are businesses in which research and development bring forth an innovative product or process. The innovation typically involves intellectual property that contributes to a strong competitive advantage in the marketplace and serves as a foundation for a high rate of growth.

Often formed around life sciences or technology innovations, these enterprises can require significant funding and specialized facilities. Owners are willing to give away equity to investors to secure the financial resources they need to grow. These businesses may cluster around research institutes and universities as technology is developed and transferred from research labs into the marketplace.

Second Stage

Second-stage enterprises have survived the startup phase and have owners who are focused on growing and expanding. The Edward Lowe Foundation defines second-stage firms as having between 10 to 99 employees and/or $1 million to $50 million in revenue.

For these companies, business plans have morphed into strategic marketing plans. Finding a location is replaced by funding an expansion. Defining a market niche transforms into finding new markets, launching a new product line, exporting or selling to the government. And finding a team to launch the business becomes a search to find the experts who can take the business to the next level.

Main Street

Main Street companies make up a large segment of the economy, serve communities' growing populations and define a community's cultural character. They often support local sports teams, are active community leaders and donate to local causes. These entrepreneurs are found among the local dry cleaner, grocery store owner, coffee shop owner, restaurateur or graphic design boutique.

Main Street entrepreneurs aren't necessarily driven by rapid growth. The founders create the businesses to build a successful career in their area of passion and expertise and plan to work in the company for a long time. Their exit plan may involve selling the company to a key employee or passing it on to a family member.

Microenterprise

According to the Association for Enterprise Opportunity (AEO), microenterprises are businesses that require less than $35,000 in capitalization to start.[10] Many of these companies are being started by freelancers, downsized workers and retirees. Often these small enterprises support each other, offering goods, services and connections to serve each other's needs around marketing, accounting, etc.

In the microenterprise space, there is a segment of nonprofit support organizations that help those in poverty build wealth through microenterprise. Referrals may come from social services agencies, and this group may need additional technical assistance due to lack of basic business operations skills.

A bit about startups

Every company goes through the startup phase. Regardless of industry or type of business, almost all startups go through the same steps: ideation, feasibility, legal formation, licensing and permits. That said, someone starting a restaurant or food truck going through those steps will need different kinds of support than someone starting a company based on a new technology. In most communities, it is helpful to route the earliest-stage startups to specific resources that specialize in the industry and that have time and resources to spend with those in the conceptual stage.

Keep in mind these are working definitions. Entrepreneurs are people, and will continually defy efforts to place them in nice neat boxes or under specific labels.

[10] Association for Enterprise Opportunity. Retrieved July 2017. http://www.resnaprojects.org/AFTAP/telework/forum09/IntroMED.pdf.

Resources for Entrepreneurs

It's not just entrepreneurs and business owners that roughly fall into these categories. Support resources tend to cluster around the different types of entrepreneurs. So if you know which resource serves which type of business owner, you can do a better job of helping people find the right resource. And you can allay some of the fears about duplication of services.

When we first started talking about mapping resources and collaborations in the Kansas City area with KCSoureLink, there was quite a bit of concern that we'd find way too much overlap in services. The truth: once we started slicing and dicing by these audiences, and by the services offered, we found very little duplication of services. True, there were lots of business planning classes. But one was geared to startups, another to second-stage, another to innovation-led businesses. Add the geographic diversity to that and it's easy to see that each resource had a specific market niche.

The benefit: when we could refer entrepreneurs to a resource that focused on their type of business, and provided the kind of service they needed, everybody won. We found much greater satisfaction from the entrepreneurs in terms of service delivery (because they were getting what they needed from a service provider that understood them) and we had more satisfaction from the resource providers because they felt better equipped to refer clients not a fit for them to another resource in the network.

Why Do Types of Entrepreneurs Matter?

We've seen many communities where much of the focus, energy and resources are directed at the innovation-led sector. From one perspective that makes sense: one of the most consistent findings of macroeconomics is that innovation drives economic growth.[11] From the standpoint of job creation, every microenterprise that gets started employs at least one person. And added together, those numbers can be significant in a community. Also, by being inclusive rather than exclusive, every resource partner can feel part of the network and every entrepreneur can feel supported.

Across the United States, here's the breakdown of the various types of entrepreneurs we've defined (Figure 4).

[11] Praxis Strategy Group. "Enterprising States." U.S. Chamber of Commerce Foundation.

	Microenterprise	77%	**23,836,937**
	Main Street	21%	**6,822,074**
	Innovation-Led	1%	**289,817**
	Second Stage	1%	**280,540**

People thinking of starting a business: **14,806,479**

Big business (employ more than 100): **170,653**

Source: U.S. Census Bureau data 2013; Kauffman Foundation/ACS Survey 2014; MERIC

Figure 4: The quadrants of entrepreneurs[12]
(companies with fewer than 100 employees)

Innovation-Led

Innovation-Led firms create high-paying jobs

Innovation-led businesses, while a very small number in the overall entrepreneurship landscape (1 percent nationally), are significant job creators. Research in the Kansas City market based on Quarterly Census of Economic Wages data shows new and young tech firms created more than 1,000 jobs in 2016, or about 7.5 percent of the jobs created by all new employers with fewer than 20 employees. And these are well-paid jobs: The average wage paid by new and young tech firms was just under $80,000, compared to an average wage of less than $50,000.

Tim Jemal works with innovation-led businesses every day. He is the executive director of the Technology Councils of North America (TECNA), representing more than 50 IT and technology trade organizations throughout the United States and Canada that work with both large and small companies.

[12] Source: Census.gov. Microenterprises are non-employer firms less innovation-led firms; Second Stage firms are a subset of firms 1-99 employees, determined by a calculation developed by MERIC (Chasing Cheetahs); Innovation-led firms are a subset of firms 1-99 employees and non-employer firms, defined by NAICS code; Main Street firms are the remaining firms 1-99 employees; Starters are determined by a calculation based on Kauffman Foundation research.

"Tech entrepreneurs are important because their ideas lead to job creation and contribute to the local, state and national economy. These are the people coming up with ideas and eventually bringing products and services to market."

Jemal helps tech councils support the innovation-led entrepreneurs in their communities.

"Tech councils can help bring to market and commercialize the innovative ideas coming from entrepreneurs. This leads to job creation and company growth. More jobs lead to larger companies, larger companies create more impact to the economy in terms of taxes and higher wages for employees."

Finding and hiring the right talent is a crucial challenge for innovation-led companies of any size.

"It's not a secret that everyone is seeking talent. Forty-one percent of U.S. IT firms reported openings and are recruiting talent. Tech councils are fantastic connectors between talent and employers. There are some excellent workforce development programs managed by local tech councils. It can be as simple as a jobs board to public/private partnerships around K-12 STEM education."

Jemal encourages economic development entities and local tech communities to take a hard look at support for innovation-led firms.

"We need to prioritize how we spend our dollars. Investing in what's working through proven organizations like tech councils makes sense. We need to do it in a way that is measured and uses programs that will have a long-term impact on growth and job-creation. Are we creating jobs?"

Second-Stage Entrepreneurs

A balanced approach to economic development

The Edward Lowe Foundation champions second-stage businesses and Penny Lewandowski has been a key evangelist for that message. Lewandowski has worked with entrepreneurs for 25 years, most recently as executive director of the Greater Baltimore Technology Council and currently as a senior consultant with the Edward Lowe Foundation, focusing on the organization's external relationships. She is known as a thought leader in entrepreneurship-led economic development, a form of economic development that focuses on growing from within, with a particular focus on second-stage growth companies.

Lewandowski believes in a balanced approach to economic development.

"Ensuring a balance between resources devoted to existing business – especially growth companies – and resources for startups and attraction is key. This kind of balance leads to more sustainable, stickier growth. A strategy focused solely on startups means long wait times for results. And a strategy focused solely on incentives is a zero-sum game when it comes to job growth. If you have a balance, you are far more poised for success.

"When economic and community developers think about entrepreneurship, they think startups. Everyone loves a 'start in the basement' story. It's exciting, and information-hungry startups are easy to serve. But Dan Isenberg (founder of the Entrepreneurial Ecosystem Platform at Babson Executive Education) says there is little evidence that stimulating startup growth leads to critical job creation.

"Growth-oriented second-stage companies, defined as having between 10 and 99 employees and annual revenues between $1 million and $50 million, are the strongest and most sustainable job creators in any community."

According to data from YourEconomy.org, between 2006 and 2016 second-stage companies in the United States represented almost 16 percent of establishments but generated 37.5 percent of all jobs and 36.3 percent of sales.

"When you see numbers like that, it's hard to understand why these companies receive less support than their startup and big-company peers. In addition to jobs, second-stagers tend to be more innovative, export products and services outside of their communities, take great care of their employees and understand the power of giving back. And if you show them your love, they're far more inclined to stay in your community when a site selector offers incentives to lure them to perceived greener pastures.

"We get so focused on big – the big win with promises of jobs that may or may not materialize – that we forget about the singles, doubles and triples these second-stage companies create. Few baseball games are won by all home runs, so from our perspective, it pays to support existing companies with an intention for growth."

A scaleup ecosystem

Verne Harnish with Gazelles Inc. and founder of ScaleUpU is a proponent of communities looking beyond just startups and innovation-led companies. He makes a strong case for supporting second stage companies that are scaling.

"There needs to be a scaleup ecosystem to augment startup ecosystems. The local

community gets led by politicians and media around large entrepreneurial firms, like Red Hat in North Carolina and Cerner in Kansas City. On the flip side, there are lots of small businesses, and techies in their 20s make a great story. But the ones who are really doing the heavy lifting are the middle market companies.

"These companies have been around for a while, they own crazy niches, they are invisible – the unsung heroes of the economy.

"That's why we started ScaleUpU, to at least shine the spotlight on them, give them the recognition they deserve. At the end of the day it's education, how to handle the various things unique to scaling a business, different than startups and different from running a large company."

Harnish believes that education is the key.

"Andreesson Horowitz, the number one VC (venture capital) firm, call themselves the non-VC venture capital firm because their big focus is identifying and teaching entrepreneurs to be CEOs rather than replacing them. That's why I started a program at MIT, Birthing of Giants, 25 years ago and I still teach it. It was all about giving entrepreneurs like Brad Feld the kind of education that he needed because he had launched a company and was scaling it."

In addition to education, coaching is critical.

"No one has ever achieved peak performance without a coach. And it takes more than one coach. It takes a village of coaches. It's what TechStars[13] *does so well with their model."*

He also shares a bit of advice for companies trying to scale.

"If you want to scale you've got to move beyond selling in the United States. We have a huge weakness, we've been so lucky (or addicted) to a fairly large market. We don't have the instincts to do business outside the United States. The new diversification strategy is along geographic lines."

Main Street Entrepreneurs

Local businesses create big impact

For every $100 spent at a local business, approximately $67 stays in the

[13] TechStars is a global accelerator program founded in Boulder, Colorado, in 2006.

community. When you shop at a big box store, just $32 out of $100 stays in the community. Only 14 jobs are created for every $10 million in consumer spending at Amazon, while 57 jobs are created for the same amount spent locally.[14]

These are just a few of the statistics presented by the Business Alliance for Local Living Economies (BALLE), and part of the reason why former BALLE Executive Director Michelle Long is passionate about being a national advocate for local business.

"Localism can start with a simple commitment to 'buy local' – keeping your dollars where your heart lives. It also means supporting your community to identify, launch and grow the businesses that are needed to serve your community.

"These businesses might be people who have a deli or a restaurant who are looking for what their community loves to eat and what makes it special or fun. They are clothing and apparel manufacturers who source their materials locally, fiber that can be grown locally, from dirt to shirt.

"Who are these businesses? They are people who have a stake in the community."

Long believes that the policies that focus on attraction of businesses into a community may not always pay off in the long run.

"There's an alternative to bringing in a branch of a multinational company to create 500 jobs in the community. More and more people are realizing that you can have 50 businesses create 10 jobs each or 100 businesses create five jobs each. These local businesses are rooted in the community and are not apt to move based on the latest subsidy.

"We're not against large businesses, but we shouldn't subsidize them and make it an uneven playing field for local people. We ask our local people to pay taxes and then we use that to subsidize companies that compete with them. That makes zero sense. I feel like local businesses are thriving and succeeding in spite of policies.

The impact of locally-owned businesses goes beyond jobs and sales.

"It's so much easier when you approach a local owner, a neighbor, (about an issue) because they can see the connections, They understand that, 'Yes we need to have healthy water and jobs for our people.' When you are in a local community, you feel more responsibility and accountability.

---

[14] Business Alliance for Local Living Economies (BALLE). Retrieved July 2017. https://bealocalist.org/.

"Local owners have freedom and autonomy and self-determination for their place and for each other. They don't wait to find out who's in charge. Too often I've seen people who work on the ground approach a branch manager about something, and the manager has to check with corporate. And then the project fizzles. With local owners, it's their choice and decision. They can take action.

"Focusing on these kinds of business ensures that lots of owners are offering their gifts and their creativity to the community and are in a relationship with the people they purchase from and who purchase from them."

Microenterprise

Many motives for microenterprise

Microbusinesses represent more than 90 percent of the small businesses in the United States. According to the Association for Enterprise Opportunity, an organization of microenterprise loan funds and supporters, microbusinesses accounted for about 26 million jobs in 2011 and had an economic impact of $4.87 trillion.[15] That same study showed microbusinesses generating $42 billion in federal taxes and $51.8 billion in state and local taxes.

In her role as AEO senior vice president for new initiatives, Tammy Halevy studies and supports this critical segment of the economy.

"We would describe microbusiness as the largest segment of small business. Microbusinesses include solo owners, businesses with up to five employees, including the owner, and a growing portion are in the gigeconomy (Uber drivers, Etsy sellers, people who are generating income from assets they have or their capabilities).

"Historically we called these businesses microenterprise. We started using microbusiness because when people think of microenterprise they think of a woman and a goat in Bangladesh."

Halevy points out that many microbusinesses operate on Main Street USA, and that microbusiness owners don't fit into a few, neat categories.

"There's a real dynamism between microbusiness and small business. We did some empirical analysis in 2013 looking at a set of microbusinesses over time. One of the

[15] Association for Enterprise Opportunity. "Bigger Than You Think: The Economic Impact of Microbusiness in the United States." Retrieved July 2017. http://www.aeoworks.org/index.php/site/page/category/reports/.

things that we found is that 15 percent grew well beyond the five employees. They didn't all set out with that aspiration.

"All kinds of people start businesses. People don't necessarily set out to have a microbusiness. They have a broad range of motivations. People have a passion, or an idea, or see an unmet need. You have people who are motivated by the notion of 'I want to be my own boss.' You hear a lot about the passion they have for building something for their children.

"Self-employment, while not easy, can be more flexible. Folks who have a passion and an income generation need can and do start as a part-time gig, test the waters while they still have another job. There are folks for whom traditional labor markets are a challenge because of some barrier to employment."

Whatever the motivation, these microbusiness owners have a macro impact.

"If you think of microbusiness compared to large corporation, it's infinitesimally small. But in the aggregate, the impact is reasonably significant. We did an economic analysis of impact a few years ago, based on 2011 data. There were 26 million direct jobs created by microbusiness owners. Then there were 1.9 million indirect jobs, contracting to others for example. And the induced effect, the economic consequences on value creation from individuals employed by microbusinesses, is 13.4 million jobs.

"There's the contribution to economic activity and local job creation. These firms tend to hire from within the community and create jobs in the vicinity. They contribute to the social fabric.

"There's also a personal satisfaction dimension ... for themselves and for their families. I would not undervalue the sense of achievement and personal satisfaction that business owners will talk about, share in focus groups and report back in survey data. I don't know how we can quantify the personal satisfaction and increased engagement."

From her vantage point, Halevy has seen many things that communities can do to encourage microbusiness.

"Lots of stakeholders can do lots of things to support microbusiness. We can make systematic investments in making capital available and the environment to support microbusinesses. We can streamline regulatory activities, make licensing easy to understand, easy to engage. We can patronize local businesses. People can make choices to shop at, use and rely on microbusinesses.

"We are seeing a lot of public spaces to support entrepreneurs. In east Austin an incubator recently opened in a deeply underserved neighborhood. For the entrepreneurs that use the space, the alternative before was having a meeting in a community center or a gym. That was not great for a business meeting. All kinds of folks who had been working in their homes, quietly pushing businesses forward, came out of the woodwork. I think there's something about physical space, something communities can do.

"Part of the challenge of supporting microbusiness is there is a lot of wheel reinventing. These needs and opportunities exist in every community. Every owner is different, but there are common needs. Every community is different, but there is commonality. Instead of taking what we have and building on it, we reinvent. Communities need to look outside, what is working elsewhere and adopt that. Whether it's the referral platform AEO is developing or SourceLink, there is a lot of commonality in this notion of creating infrastructure. Finding ways to deliver what businesses need in an efficient way is very important."

The Promise of Minority Entrepreneurship

Minority entrepreneurs can be found in every quadrant of entrepreneurship. National expert Dell Gines believes entrepreneurship offers a promise to minority communities for advancement.

Gines is passionate about supporting economic growth through entrepreneurship with a specific focus on small rural and urban core communities. He's a senior community development advisor for the Federal Reserve Bank of Kansas City and a leading researcher and speaker on minority entrepreneurship.

He believes that entrepreneurship holds the key to creating equality in minority communities.

"I personally think entrepreneurship is the most critical issue in minority communities. The black and white income gap is the highest it's been since 1979. That's roughly the same income gap we had immediately after civil rights in the 1960s.

"The promise of integration and civil rights was that the gaps would close. My argument is that this arises from a deficit in the creation of local businesses in black neighborhoods. When you look at it from that standpoint, you can see entrepreneurship as a way of closing the wealth gap. If you asked most people from an African-American community to list the top five priorities, getting more entrepreneurs is lowest or not on the list.

"You have to grow your way out of these low income communities. In inner cities that are black or brown, the current model of economic development has proven not to address the concerns of those communities. A large part of that is because local entrepreneurship and local ownership is required to build local wealth and local opportunities."

Building Confidence for Women Entrepreneurs

Women entrepreneurs hit the 10 million mark in 2012, according to the National Women's Business Council, and are starting 1,200 businesses a day.[16] Women owned 36 percent of all non-farm businesses and those businesses generated $1.6 trillion in total receipts and employed 8.9 million.

Sherry Turner has been working with women entrepreneurs across the spectrum for the past 13 years. Her organization, OneKC for Women, encompasses education and access to loans through the Kansas City Women's Business Center and the WE-Lend microloan program; equity investing through the Women's Capital Connection; and economic empowerment through the Women's Employment Network. She sees many areas where men and women entrepreneurs are the same.

"Successful entrepreneurs don't see anything as a barrier, and that's certainly true in the women's space. When you sit down and consult with these folks, you can see the difference. Those that are highly successful have a very positive and optimistic viewpoint about what's in front of them. Those who are struggling have an excuse for why the business is not moving forward.

"Access to capital is an issue for all entrepreneurs. You can always find somebody who's behind the times, who is discriminatory, but as a whole, financial institutions are really looking at the loan application, do you or don't you have the credit or the capacity to repay the loan.

"The data supports that women don't initially have the networks and connectivity that sometimes can make or break a startup. What we can do from the Women's Business Center is to make a referral. We can say 'go to this person at this bank.' And we don't make the referral if they aren't ready. In the last few years, we've really concentrated on the financial piece, making sure our women entrepreneurs are comfortable with understanding their financials, understanding their inventory and cash flow. If you know that, then you're going to be able to articulate to a banker what the banker needs to know.

[16] National Women's Business Council. "10 Million Strong – The Tipping Point for Women's Entrepreneurship," 2015. Retrieved July 2017. https://www.nwbc.gov/research/the-tipping-point.

"There's no doubt, there are areas of gender difference. The way women learn, the confidence levels are different. Women need to be more educated before we feel we are confident. Men typically go for it even if they are faking the education piece. They are more confident and optimistic out of the chute.

"A women's business center is a comfortable space where a woman can get that education, can navigate what she doesn't know. Especially at the early stages of developing a business, confidence building for women is really important, and that's where the education comes in.

"I also think the data shows that women-owned businesses are much smaller. I see so much of that is by choice. Women make decisions from a very holistic viewpoint. Motherhood, care for the elderly ... women consider how it will affect the entire family environment. Many women choose to scale their businesses after their children are older and they don't have as many commitments.

"I applaud women who make an educated decision about starting or scaling a business. We've been teaching FastTrac® (a business development class) since I've been here. About 50 percent who take the class actually launch within a year. Many make the educated decision that it's not the right time for them. I think it's wonderful that they invest in the exploration."

In addition to working with women-led companies, Turner also works with women investors.

"We started Women's Capital Connection because of the huge gap in equity funding. We're now in our tenth year and our pipeline is full. We've been educating women entrepreneurs about this kind of capital, helping them feel comfortable enough to scale. We've also been educating women about how to invest in early-stage companies. When we started, we were one of six angel groups of women entrepreneurs investing in women-led companies. Now we are one of 17.

"None of us working here have much sympathy around some of the stereotypes about women entrepreneurs, the self-proclaimed prophecies. A barrier is just a hurdle."

A Note on Rural Enterprises

Rural enterprises can be any of the above. Focus groups conducted in communities across Missouri revealed additional issues faced by rural entrepreneurs:

- A sense of isolation, both from other entrepreneurs and from the larger business and political community
- Lack of knowledge about emerging markets
- Lack of access to capital
- Limited understanding about available business support services and how to use them

In *Strengthening Local Rural Economies through Entrepreneurs,* Brian Dabson expands on the challenges to rural entrepreneurs. Low population size and density, and as a consequence, limited local demand, make it difficult for rural businesses to achieve economies of scale or critical mass. Entrepreneurs in rural communities are less likely to find the resources and services that are taken for granted in more urban locations:

- Regular parcel services
- High-speed Internet access
- Utilities may be hard to find
- Rural lending institutions
- Specialist technical advice
- Suitable buildings with the right access, configuration[17]

In rural communities, there are few lending institutions. This frequently limits access to capital. Limited competition may also encourage risk averse behaviors on the part of lenders. Moreover, entrepreneurs are less likely to encounter peers with whom they can share ideas and problems – the absence of support networks may limit levels of new firm creation.[18]

Regional alliances that connect communities together electronically and through physical events can increase access to resources, including capital, and provide opportunities for face-to-face interactions. Networked infrastructure can lessen the sense of isolation, make visible resources that are distant yet available and broaden the diversity of those who choose to start and grow businesses in rural communities.

Entrepreneurship on the Frontier

Erik Monsen, associate professor at the University of Vermont Grossman School of Business in Burlington, has been collecting stories of

[17] Brian Dabson. "Strengthening Local Rural Economies through Entrepreneurs." The American Midwest: Managing Change in Rural Transition, 2002.

[18] Ibid.

entrepreneurship on the frontier between rural and metropolitan areas.

"We know a lot about Silicon Valley and Boston and New York, but what about these frontier regions?

"A lot of people want to live someplace smaller, close to nature, know their neighbors. Traditional large corporations like IBM used to be big here, but that is no longer the case. People say, 'If I want to live in Vermont, I'll need to start my own company and make my own job.'

"Two students in the business school, Max Robbins and Peter Silverman, tell the story of how they wanted internships in Vermont in the summer, but they couldn't find them. They realized 'If we can't find an internship, maybe we have to start a company to help other students find internships.' And that's what they did, which resulted in an innovative company initially named Beacon and now MajorWise (www.getmajorwise.com).

"It morphed from internships and longer term jobs to projects and mini jobs. Their research showed that the current generation of students doesn't want to commit to a long internship and small businesses don't have the money or patience for a three-month internship. Thus, students can work for two-three weeks in the small business and practice new skills, and the small business can get the brochure or website they need at a reasonable price.

The nice thing about Vermont is that people who want to be here also want to work together. Students from big cities are initially protective of their ideas. Here in Vermont you don't have to be protective. You want to tell people about your idea because this is the best way to find the help you need to build your company. We have a very collaborative culture here in Vermont. We have harsh winters and if your neighbor needs help shoveling out, you help them shovel out because you may need their help. Everyone wants to help each other, because they all want to live and do well here.

"A lot of creating an entrepreneurial ecosystem outside of a big city comes down to creating easy-to-find spaces, and putting resources in place that entrepreneurs can pick up and use, like a maker space (Generator https://generatorvt.com/) or a coworking space (VCET http://vermonttechnologies.com/). It takes a little infrastructure but it makes it easier for makers and entrepreneurs to find each other and bounce against each other. And building bridges to local universities, like the University of Vermont, who have pioneering technologies and very smart students, can help to turbo charge the process."

Leadership tip:

Don't get into fights and don't spend a lot of time defining the terms of what's an entrepreneur. There is no right answer at the back of the book.

Come up with a working definition of entrepreneur that fits your community and get started. The more inclusive the definition, the more comprehensive your entrepreneurial infrastructure will be.

Entrepreneurs are of wide variety and resources cluster around the type of entrepreneurs they serve. How do you identify and connect them together?

Section 2

3. IDENTIFY

"Win where you stand."
-Clifton Taulbert, *Who Owns the Icehouse* 2010

The hardest part of any journey is figuring out where to start. A great place to start building your entrepreneurial infrastructure is right where you are, right now. That means you need a clear picture of where your community is, right now. What are the assets? What support mechanisms for entrepreneurs and business owners are in place? Are they connected? What are the gaps?

Mapping the entrepreneurial support assets in a community is both easy and hard. It's easy to put together a list of what programs are out there. Just search Google for entrepreneurship or "startup + your community" and see what you get. It's hard to talk with the resource providers, get to know what they do and who they serve, understand at a deep level their strengths, challenges, concerns and opportunities.

You'll find many benefits to starting where you are. First, where else can you start? Second, by recognizing that there are already resources in the community on which to build, you will respect the work that has gone before and ruffle fewer feathers. And make no mistake, someone (or several someones) in your community has been working to help entrepreneurs and business owners. Chances are, they are pretty invisible because they don't have the resources or staff to market effectively.

This approach was validated by author and economist Philip Auerswald in a report commissioned by the Kauffman Foundation in 2015.

"Map the ecosystem. Create an inventory or graph that indicates who the participants in the ecosystem are and how they are connected. More ambitiously, map roles and differentiate relationships by type, direction and magnitude of interaction. Once validated by the entrepreneurs and community members, ecosystem maps can become valuable tools in developing strategies for engagement."[19]

[19] Philip Auerswald. "Enabling Entrepreneurial Ecosystems." Ewing Marion Kauffman Foundation, 2015.

Step by Step: Mapping Your Assets

At SourceLink we've worked with a number of communities to map their entrepreneurial assets. It's not rocket science.

1. Find a few like-minded people in the entrepreneurial community … entrepreneurs, resource providers, community supporters: this will be your core team.
2. As a core team, list the resources you know that support entrepreneurs and small business owners. Keep in mind that it's not just about supporting innovation-led businesses. List the full range of resources, from microloans and credit-building services to high-tech incubators and venture pitch programs.
   Note that several national programs frequently have a local presence: SCORE, FastTrac®, Small Business Development Centers, 1 Million Cups and more.
3. Start pulling those people together. Ask them about the challenges and opportunities in your community. Ask them who else should be included in these conversations.
4. Rinse and repeat.

Many communities have an abundance of business development resources, but often entrepreneurs can't find them or they reach out to one that's not a good fit and have a bad experience. With the multitude of different kinds of businesses – whether they are innovation-led, Main Street, second stage or microenterprise – and a multitude of resources available to serve them, a central point for visibility and connection can help strengthen businesses and accelerate their growth.

Starting KCSourceLink

It was exactly that situation that led to the start of KCSourceLink. The Ewing Marion Kauffman Foundation is based in Kansas City and by the early 2000s had begun to build a reputation in entrepreneurship. The only challenge was that the foundation didn't offer technical services directly to the entrepreneur. People called all the time asking for help to start or expand their businesses. They called asking for money. They called to find mentors.

Staff at the foundation knew the resources to address these issues were already in the community because the foundation was funding most of them. Clearly there was a disconnect between the people who needed the help and the resource organizations that offered the services.

To validate the point, focus groups with entrepreneurs were conducted. The message was consistent: "We know there are resources to help us, we just don't know which one to go to or how to find the right one." The focus groups also picked up another challenge: the resource providers did not know much about each other, and therefore did not make quality referrals to each other. One person described it as "BBs in a box car," with the entrepreneur being bounced from one organization to the next.

The solution: the Kauffman Foundation partnered with the University of Missouri–Kansas City and the local U.S. Small Business Administration office to create a "one-stop shop" for all entrepreneurial services. The project built on some earlier work by then UMKC Professor Patricia Greene (now at Babson College). At least that was the original vision. But like in any good entrepreneurial endeavor, the KCSourceLink leadership team pivoted to a networked model, with KCSourceLink in the center as a kind of "switching station."

KCSourceLink was formed in 2003 to connect individuals, organizations and institutions that support entrepreneurship to one another and to the community at large. KCSourceLink helps thousands of entrepreneurs and business owners each year gain access to the right resource at the right time through a hotline, a website, the community's most comprehensive business events calendar, active social media, events and more.

Today, KCSourceLink is in the middle of a thriving entrepreneurial network that links more than 240 resources in support of every type of entrepreneur in an 18-county metro area. But it didn't start there. And it certainly didn't stop there.

It started in an abandoned classroom with 25 desks, a chalkboard and no phone line.

We started KCSourceLink by doing exactly what we described earlier in our steps for mapping assets. We invited a group of resource providers to a meeting. We plied them with cookies and coffee. We asked them a few key questions:

- What are the strengths of Kansas City's entrepreneurial community?

- What is unique about Kansas City's entrepreneurial community?
- What is the greatest challenge for local entrepreneurs?
- What is the greatest challenge for you, the service provider?
- What services do you provide to entrepreneurs and what kind of entrepreneurs are you best positioned to serve?
- Who else should we talk to?

We did that several times, with several groups of service providers. After we asked them questions, we told them about what we were trying to do, how we wanted to help them connect to each other through a network. We described the benefits of a network (better visibility, better referrals, better outcomes.) We patiently explained that we were not here to steal all their clients and suck up all the funding dollars in the community. We told this story over and over again, in small groups and one-on-one meetings. Some of the resource providers got it immediately, jumped in and became our team members in recruiting others. Some were hesitant, reluctant and down-right hostile.

Our best defense was the way we approached the project: with the resource providers as a key customer. The entrepreneurs that would benefit from the network were certainly a customer as well, but we thought of resource providers as our equals.

Since our resource providers were our customers, we took great care in thinking about how we interacted with them. We worked diligently to make sure that each partner got appropriate referrals, and we were not seen as favoring one over another. At every opportunity we tried to lead from behind, and let the spotlight shine on the resource providers. When there were opportunities for joint projects, we made sure to share the funding when possible.

We also took the time to understand at a deep level what each organization did and what audience it served. This helped us connect people to the right resource at the right time, play into the strengths of the resource providers and increase the chance of the entrepreneur being satisfied with the service provided.

Taking the Show on the Road

We continued that work, taking the SourceLink model to other communities and helping them build their entrepreneurial infrastructure from the ground up. SourceLink staff have facilitated these kinds of discussions in Columbus, Dallas, Denver, Phoenix, San Juan, Seattle, Tampa Bay, among others. The strengths and unique assets are just that: unique to each community. What's really interesting is that the challenges to entrepreneurs and to the entrepreneurial support organizations tend to be the same, regardless of community size or geography.

Reports that summarize the findings provided a focal point for continuing the conversation in the community. Our partners in those communities used the reports to reach beyond the initial participants to get feedback, encourage others to get involved and convince potential funders of the needs and the opportunities.

Sharing the Asset Map

As we said, it's hard to map the assets in your community. But it's worth it. Because once you have the "map" of assets you can share the information in a number of creative ways.

Create posters to make the assets more visible

JPMorgan Chase wanted to do something significant to support entrepreneurs in a few of their markets. They were interested in doing something that would have value beyond just the week of Startup Week (of which they were national sponsors), and would also reach beyond the innovation-led companies.

JPMorgan Chase decided to map the assets in six cities and make those resources visible through a printed piece called SourceFinder℠. The SourceFinder poster categorized the entrepreneurship support resources in each community by stage of business and by service offered.

SourceLink worked closely with JPMorgan Chase community advocates in Columbus, Phoenix, Denver, Seattle, Tampa Bay and Dallas–Fort Worth. We searched databases, held meetings and called people on the phone to gather intelligence on each resource depicted on the SourceFinder.

The result was a customized poster for each community, with four of the communities electing to also launch an online database using The Resource Navigator® tool.

Build a statewide collaboration

The Virginia Community Economic Network partnered with SourceLink in 2014 to map their entrepreneurial assets and make them more visible. They chose to use The Resource Navigator®, an online database that allows entrepreneurs to search for assistance by stage of business, industry and area of assistance (Figure 5).

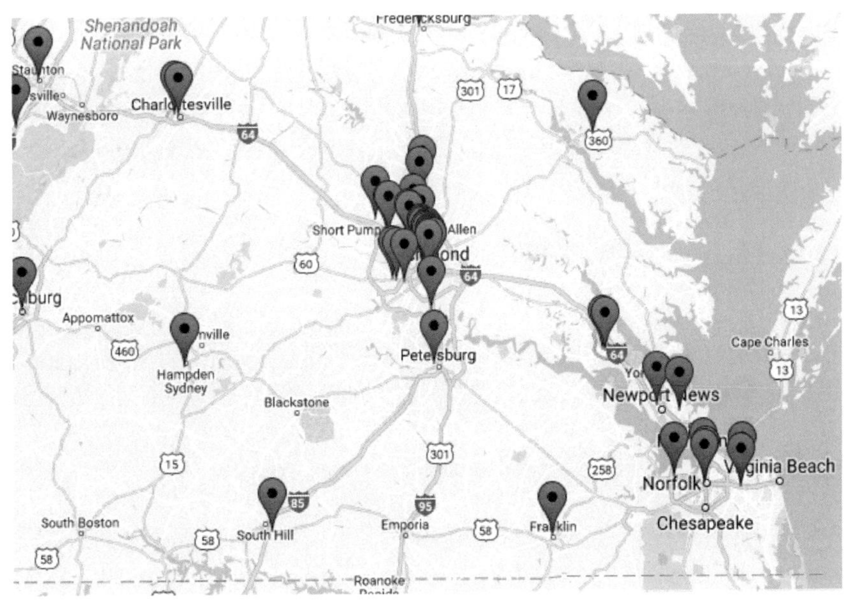

Figure 5: VCEN network mapped using The Resource Navigator

Conaway Haskins III, with the Virginia Cooperative Extension at Virginia Tech, leads SourceLink Virginia. He talks about why the state turned its attention to entrepreneurship.

"Our state has been heavily reliant on the federal government. We are right next door to Washington, D.C. The Pentagon is in Virginia. But even before federal cutbacks, the leadership at the state level felt there needed to be a change in economic development. The challenge is, if you've been doing it one way for 50 or 60 years, making the shift is not easy.

"The previous and current governors both identified entrepreneurship and innovation as top line priorities. They saw the need to diversify the Virginia economy. Essentially we have two states in one, the suburbs or northern Virginia (NOVA) and the rest of Virginia (ROVA). Virginia is in the top 15 states economically, but it you take NOVA out, the rest of the state looks much like other southern states.

"The other parts of the state were more distressed and were looking at entrepreneurship for a while. They influenced state policy makers to start looking, too.

"At first, we were simply trying to figure out what was already going on in the entrepreneurship and small business space ... what are we doing, what programs we have, what's coming out of various state departments. We wanted to do an inventory of state programs around entrepreneurship and small business."

Once Virginia got The Resource Navigator database up and running, they worked with several key partners across the state to load the search tool onto their websites, expanding the availability and visibility to more entrepreneurs. Haskins talks about the challenge of building those collaborations.

"Building collaborations is very difficult. There's a natural tendency to not collaborate. People were frustrated and couldn't find one central place to find all the programs for entrepreneurs and small business. Because no one was doing it, there was a gap, no one had ownership. We were able to fill that gap. It became easier and clearer, but it still took time.

"You have to spend a lot of time meeting with key individuals who can be helpful, meeting with key individuals who are potential underminers. You have to establish a personal rapport on an individual basis. You can't convene people if they aren't interested, and you can't find the interest if they don't have a sense of buy-in. You have to have those relationships built and you have to spend time on it.

"It's incredibly important to be neutral, and (being neutral is) incredibly underestimated and incredibly hard. Being neutral doesn't mean not having an opinion. At some point you have to have definitive views and a task. You have to help people see the higher purpose.

"Working at the state level takes commitment. You can't run an entrepreneurial ecosystem if you're not there. We're supporting existing and emerging regional efforts. We have the information about who's doing what. That tends to be the biggest local hurdle. We've mapped the resources, taken that off the plate, so the local folks can focus on the relationship building."

Develop a map of resources

In Kansas City, we launched The Resource Navigator early in the process. But people still wanted a hard-copy map in addition to the online search capability. They wanted something they could touch and feel. With more than 240 resources, a poster was not the answer.

KCSourceLink's communications team came up with the Resource Rail℠ (Figure 6), with a nod to the area's newly launched streetcar line. The Resource Rail is a graphic map that visualizes the many resources that serve all different types of entrepreneurs. The information gathered from each Resource Partner was used to determine where each would be placed on the "streetcar" line. The colored lines indicate the type of entrepreneur served (microenterprise, Main Street, innovation-led, second stage) and the stops indicate the stages a business goes through and the assistance available along the way.

Entrepreneurs and business owners rely on their social networks for success. You can strengthen and support networks by connecting the entrepreneurship support resources you've identified in your community.

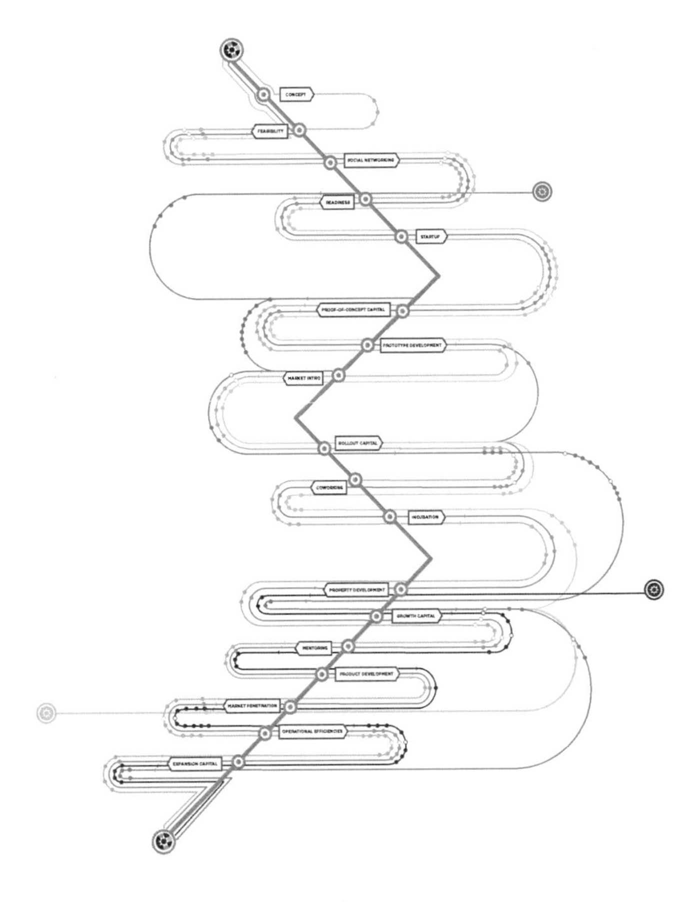

Source: www.kcsourcelink.com/resource-rail

Figure 6: KCSourceLink Resource Rail℠

Leadership tip:

The work of building an entrepreneurial infrastructure is incredibly fulfilling and can make a marked difference to the entrepreneurs in your community. But it's not easy. Be prepared for the negative, from outright slings and arrows to the more subtle forms of harassment (backbiting, undercutting.) Early on we heard Resource Partners declare that our intention was to "take them out of business" and that "we'll keep all the clients for ourselves" and that "we'll be competing for funding."

Our best response was to explain the program, describe the benefits, and, once we had some history, point to what we had done.

Eventually it got better.

But we did have that one service provider who absolutely, positively refused to participate. We didn't get them to sign on for the KCSourceLink network until the original director moved on.

Patience is a virtue.

Now that you know how to map the assets in your entrepreneurial community, start connecting those assets. Start the conversation, pull people together, understand what's going on in your community so you can build a strong, visible network.

4. CONNECT

"Successful entrepreneurs are not necessarily smarter, just better connected to and through the ecosystem."

-Jeff Tucker, Advanced Manufacturing Institute, Kansas State University

"Entrepreneurs need connections."

-Jeff Hoffman, founder of PriceLine

Edward Glaeser in *The Triumph of the City* says, "In America and Europe, cities speed innovation by connecting their smart inhabitants to each other."

In Regional Advantage: Culture and Competition in Silicon Valley and Route 128 (1996), Analee Saxenian makes the case that the connected and open network of Silicon Valley enabled it to emerge more successful over the siloed approach of Route 128 in Boston.

"The informal socializing that grew out of these quasi familial relationships supported the ubiquitous practices of collaboration and sharing of information among local producers … By all accounts, these informal conversations were pervasive and served as an important source of up-to-date information about competitors, customers, markets and technologies. Entrepreneurs came to see social relationships and even gossip as a crucial aspect of their business."

Several academic studies[20] prove what can be seen every day in working with entrepreneurs: entrepreneurs and business owners at every stage rely heavily on their social networks. These networks provide trusted referrals to funding sources for loans and equity; first customers (as well as ongoing customers); and mentors/technical experts that can support the business.

Linking together existing resources can go a long way in engaging your community and building these valuable networks. You learned how to

[20] Focusing on social network analysis turns attention to relationships between entrepreneurs and others that provide the resources that are important in establishing a business (Johannisson, 1988; Larson, 1991). Entrepreneurs have ideas to test, and some knowledge and competence to run the business, but they also need complementary resources to produce and deliver their goods or services (Teece, 1987). They get support, knowledge and access to distribution channels through their social networks. Entrepreneurs are also linked to people and organizations that interact among themselves, and these contacts can widen the availability of resources that sustain a new firm (Hansen, 1995).

"map" the assets in your community in the last chapter. Now start pulling them together. Set up a meeting, invite everyone and start a conversation about the strengths of the entrepreneurship support network, the challenges for both entrepreneurs and resource providers, what's unique about your community.

Bringing your entrepreneurial support organizations together in face-to-face gatherings can rapidly engage a broad community. Each resource provider will have its own network of entrepreneurs and support resources. You're beginning to link those networks, and interlocking networks are a powerful thing.

Not everyone can or will come to your first meeting. Have another one. Keep talking.

Step by Step: Connecting Your Resources

1. Connect the resources to each other
2. Connect resources to entrepreneurs
3. Build relationships
4. Identify opportunities for collaboration

The Benefits of Connections

Mapping the resources is only the first step in building a strong entrepreneurial infrastructure. It takes time and energy to create a strong, connected network. The benefits of making these connections outweighs the challenges. Great things can happen when the resources that support entrepreneurs are linked together.

At first, it's just getting to know each other. That in and of itself has great value. When we started holding meetings with the service providers in Kansas City (we call them Resource Partners), we saw three really good things happen.

1. Resource Partners became much better equipped to refer clients to each other. The "BBs in a boxcar" effect faded away.
2. Resource Partners became more focused on their own niche services. Prior to KCSourceLink, when a resource organization encountered a client that needed help beyond the resource's scope

of work, the resource frequently tried to add that service. The network helped the resource organization find help for the client.

3. Resource Partners started offering joint programs and collaborating on projects to fill gaps in entrepreneurial services, raise visibility for those services and seek funding.

This all benefits the entrepreneur. A connected network makes it easier for entrepreneurs to tap into the assistance they need. The entrepreneurs don't need to know every resource and every moving piece and part of the network. Sometimes this is called "no wrong door." In a connected entrepreneurial network, an entrepreneur can walk in any door of any support organization and get access to the help he or she needs.

Don Macke, Deb Markley and John Fulwider of the Center for Rural Entrepreneurship further explain this concept in *Energizing Entrepreneurial Communities: A Pathway to Prosperity:*

"… we propose a 'no wrong door' rather than a 'one-step shop' approach to market outreach. The 'no wrong door' approach requires effective networking within the community. All support providers must be familiar with the work of their partners so that effective referrals are made. Under this approach, multiple entry points create pathways into the resource system and help direct the entrepreneur to the quickest possible answer."

Simply said, by connecting resources, you've expanded the social networks for the entrepreneurs in your community.

Roping resources in western Kansas

Steve Radley, founder and CEO of NetWork Kansas, knows a bit about wrangling resources. NetWork Kansas works to encourage entrepreneurs across Kansas, working with more than 500 resource organizations. Getting all those people on board was not easy.

"Back in fall 2005, I traveled to WaKeeney to meet with an alliance representing 53 western Kansas counties. In presenting to the Western Kansas Rural Economic Development Alliance, we hoped to get enough buy-in that most would join the network of resources and help us find additional partners in the area."

Radley presented *"my slick PowerPoint presentation … Afterward, no one asked any questions and the group took a break. It had not gone well."*

"The meeting proved pivotal for us. We didn't realize it at the time, but like many other organizations, we had shown up to offer a technical solution tools and resources to a group that had seen them all. Now we saw, for the first time, how we were being perceived. We realized that our approach wouldn't have the impact that we wanted unless we gave a lot more consideration to local engagement.

"So we set out to engage partners and communities by relying on them; empower them with assets; and push decision-making away from us. We moved from short-term projects to long-term processes and from trying to have all of the answers to asking more questions."

All the hard work and effort has paid off.

"Since 2008, our flagship approach, the Entrepreneurship (E-) Community Partnership has grown from six to 59 communities. It provides communities with a locally controlled loan fund to assist entrepreneurs and small business owners with capital and connectivity to resources. And in our relationship with the western Kansas alliance, we've gone from being strangers to being friends, with 24 of our E-Communities hailing from the region. They have become one of our most valuable connecting points, representing multiple communities and network partners."

The western Kansas E-Communities have provided more than $7.48 million in matching loans to 204 businesses that created and/or retained 1,900+ jobs. Most of those loans are in communities with populations of 10,000 or fewer.

Building Relationships

It's not enough to have a list of resources or "enroll" organizations in a network. You have to build relationships with the people in the network. It requires listening and learning what each organization does, what it does well, how they are measured and what's in it for them to be working collaboratively.

In Kansas City, KCSourceLink, has a significant conversation with each partner in the network at least once a year. Of course, because we hold regular gatherings we see many of our partners much more frequently. Building relationships does several things.

- It helps us continue our learning about resources so that we can make the best referrals for both the partner and the entrepreneur.

- Turnover in nonprofits is high, so we keep tabs on newcomers and those who have left.
- Frequent conversations with a variety of groups helps us keep our finger on the pulse of what's happening – what are the emerging issues, what's going really well, where are the gaps.

As Conaway Haskins of Virginia said earlier, *"You have to have those relationships built and you have to spend time on them."*

Building a network in Iowa

The Iowa staff had a similar adventure in putting together IASourceLink: building a network of resources across the entire state. Amy Kuhlers, program manager for IASourceLink, tells how they took their show on the road.

"Basically a person got in a car.

"We made appointments for everyone we thought would be the most referred to resources. We definitely went around to the SBDCs (Small Business Development Centers), for example, organizations that we were certainly going to be working with. Along that road trip, we caught some others – chambers of commerce, community economic development directors, as well as other state agencies.

"After that, it's been an ongoing process to reach out to providers, sending emails, recruiting via phone calls. But the platform was the road trip."

Amy said building the statewide network was made easier by the fact that SourceLink already existed in Central Iowa. *"We had the Des Moines area already populated."* She said it wasn't difficult to get people to meet, *"it was more the logistics of trying to line up the appointments."*

For Amy, relationships are the key to making it work.

"We did get some resistance, and we continue to get some who see it as the state coming in and trying to find out what business contacts they have."

Amy sums up her response to resistance in three words: *"Relationship, relationship, relationship. I belong to the association of professional economic developers in the state, which is where the local developers gather. When you are part of that it gives you credibility. Additionally, I go to conferences and sponsor them, continue to meet individually with resource providers and collaborate as much as possible with other organizations. Our partnership with the University of Northern Iowa's Center for Business Growth and Innovation provides another excellent outlet for growing relationships and building program awareness."*

Iowa was motivated to build a network of resources by legislative constituents.

"In 2010, the state legislature drafted a bill that included a mandate for the then Iowa Department of Economic Development to establish a statewide network connecting entrepreneurs to available resources. Legislators were responding to constituents who were having a hard time identifying or getting access to small business resources. That was the initial push, so the legislators could say to their constituents there's one place to go."

What has Amy learned in her years with IASourceLink?

"It's always surprising to me that people still don't know where to go to get the help they need. I guess it's because I wear my economic development hat and sometimes forget to take it off. That's why you have to continue to be out there – marketing, marketing, marketing. Going out

The impact of the right resource

"It takes a village to raise a company," according to Patricia Blakely with The Merchants Fund. The Merchants Fund is a Philadelphia charity established in 1854 to provide financial assistance to current and past merchants in Philadelphia.

The work of The Merchants Fund is illustrated by the story of Marc Coleman at the Tactile Group.

The Tactile Group is a certified minority and LGBT business enterprise that designs digital products and develops custom software applications. Early on the company was in line for their first large government contract but couldn't secure a line of credit from traditional sources to add resources/ infrastructure necessary to fulfill the contract. Luckily, they were connected to the right resource with The Merchants Fund.

Coleman was working from a single room in downtown Philadelphia with a small staff. The Merchants Fund gave him $10,000 to purchase the equipment he needed to grow his business. After receiving this grant he successfully secured additional capital from other sources to help fuel the growth of his company. The business is now in its third location as a result of its success and growth.

"Awhile back Coleman found a file with all the rejection letters he received. Included in the file was a letter of acceptance from The Merchants Fund. Stories like these remind me of the importance to our work helping improve the local economy," Blakely said.

and building those relationships. I think we've benefitted from a quarterly resource partner newsletter and monthly newsletter to businesses. We like to stay in front of them."

Creating a Central Point of Contact

A central hub can help link entrepreneurs to resources, resources to other resources, entrepreneurs to other entrepreneurs. The network can be expanded to include the academic and research community, large corporations and civic leadership, building a cohesive community to support new business growth.

Someone, somewhere is answering a phone in your community to help direct entrepreneurs to resources. Why not formalize that? Implementing a one-stop phone number is a great way to promote a single contact point as well as collect information that puts you at the center of the ecosystem, letting you collect valuable information on resources' strengths, satisfaction levels and gaps. And, who wouldn't want to talk to a real person?

You may want to consider adding a central website as another way of linking the resources and making them more visible. In Kansas City, we built the KCSourceLink website as a focal point to work in conjunction with our hotline. Baltimore SourceLink, IASourceLink (Iowa), Colmena66 (Puerto Rico) and others have followed the same model.

The website allows entrepreneurs to search for resources 24/7 through The Resource Navigator tool. We have a central calendar that features events, classes and trainings from all 240 partners in the KCSourceLink network. It's one of the most visited pages on the website. We also tell the stories of local entrepreneurs and Resource Partners through a blog and a section called "Entrepreneurs in Action."

We also learned that we couldn't just put up a website and hope the world would come visit. The desire to drive significant traffic to both the hotline and the website led to an investment in marketing, especially social media. We'll talk more about that later in "Telling the Story."

Connecting Entrepreneurs: A Tale of Two Cities

While it's critical to connect the resources in a community, it's also vital to connect the entrepreneurs to each other. 1 Million Cups may be one of the best mechanisms to accomplish those connections. Robert Litan from Wichita, Kansas, and John Machacek from Fargo, North Dakota, share their stories.

Wichita

Robert Litan has been working in the entrepreneurship space since he joined the Kauffman Foundation as vice president of entrepreneurship research and now as a partner with the law firm Korein Tillery. He ascribes to Brad Feld's description of entrepreneurs as leaders and entrepreneurial supporters as feeders.

"When I started this work in 2003, incubators were around and they were really a real estate play. They weren't feeders, just places to hang out.

"Since then, the two most important developments have been accelerators and 1 Million Cups … 1MC is the institutionalization of Brad Feld's book."

Litan was working at the Kauffman Foundation when 1MC was born.

"I credit Nate Olsen with the idea … it was just a brainstorm that we (the Kauffman Foundation) piloted and all of a sudden it took off. Today it's in over 90 cities.

"I can tell you, 1MC changes everything."

More connections

As an economic development coordinator for the City of Riverside in Southern California, Steve Massa prioritizes creating networks for people and businesses to connect and find resources.

"Facilitating the right connection at the right time is the best way to add value for your community. You never know when the right connection will be made."

He tells the story of one successful connection involving two technical co-founders, Judd Lillestrand and Matt Goatcher, who connected at Riverside I/O, a local co-working/hackerspace in Riverside.

As a result of that connection, Lillestrand and Goatcher formed a new company called Bitpeel that develops custom software solutions. Massa was working with the owner of a local event planning company called LocalBoy that was looking for a new website and scheduling application.

The connection between LocalBoy and Bitpeel was so successful, the principals decided to form a third company called Check Cherry that has built a cloud-based application for DJs and other vendors in the entertainment industry.

Litan explains how 1MC transformed the Wichita entrepreneurial community.

"1MC is such a simple idea: weekly coffee. You need 6-10 people who are organizers. Everything is a formula, you have to adhere to all the guidelines if you are going to have the Kauffman imprimatur. There are two presenters, 6 minute talks, 20 minutes of Q&A, always a last question about what does the entrepreneur need from the community. It's not supposed to be pitch sessions for money. They are supposed to be 'Here's my business in a nutshell and here's my problem, can you help me solve it.'

"The first thing, 1MC helps the entrepreneurs who present. They change business plans, change business models in response to feedback, get ideas. And for the people who attend there's the peer effect. They see other people like them, they get the idea that if X can do that, I can do that. Then there's a huge networking component. People in the audience communicate with each other, meet with each other. There's a wide age range and all kinds of businesses.

"You add all those factors, that helps you begin. Wichita was unconnected and now we're a connected entrepreneurial community. I think it's the hottest thing from an entrepreneurial point of view in the city.

"I can't believe it hasn't helped every city that's active with it. We don't have studies, but we have anecdotal experience in Wichita, we know that a number of these guys have grown entirely because of 1MC."

Two companies that have presented at Wichita's 1MC stand out.

"BuddyRest is a mattress for dogs. The founder, Trevor Crotts, used to be in the mattress business. Now he's taking what he learned there and applying it to dogs, mostly older and large dogs. He's expanding to a second line of dog beds and adding toys that will stimulate the minds of older dogs.

"Illuminations makes a light that is beautiful, covered in stained glass. It hooks to your computer and your grandma's. Then you turn your light on, it will light up in another person's place. It's just a way of letting someone know you are thinking of them without saying a word."

To get 1MC going in Wichita required a major donation from Martin Pringle, a leading law firm in the community, and several people kicking in $500 each. Wichita State University has been providing space, but 1MC will be moving to a larger venue. Two coffee places donate the coffee. *"And that's not a small thing, because we average 100 to 150 people a week."*

According to Litan, 1MC led to the development of an accelerator in Wichita, which works with several growth-oriented businesses, including a few who presented at 1MC.

"E2E had six-eight companies in the first class. There are two really successful companies. One is a coffee company that is expanding to multiple locations, adding event space and exporting out of Wichita. Another is Kingfit. It is for people with diabetes, gives them a web-based place to track various measures. Their doctors follow them and give them reminders. He was going directly to patients, but changed the model and is now going through doctors."

Litan suggests that 1MC couldn't have happened at a better time.

"We're basically a manufacturing town, built around the airline industry. We used to be an entrepreneurial city and a breeding ground for franchise operations. Pizza Hut started here, Rent-a-Center started here. But we're struggling. If it weren't for the entrepreneurial activity this would be a dead town. And we're only beginning."

Fargo

You may not know much more about Fargo, North Dakota, than what was in the movie, *Fargo*. And that would be a shame, because they've got a thriving entrepreneurial and economic scene, according to John Machacek, senior vice president of finance and entrepreneurial development for the Greater Fargo Moorhead EDC.

"We've been around for 70 years and we've always done traditional economic development. While we still recruit new business to town, entrepreneurial support has taken on a bigger focus."

About five years ago the organization became more intentional about reaching out to entrepreneurs, and gave Machacek the job of entrepreneurial development.

"I'm kind of like a community concierge. I try to meet as many entrepreneurs as I can. I listen and learn about them. I have a good memory and build a database in my head about what they need or people they can help. Based on their needs, I can connect them to certain programs. Or I'll run into someone six months later who can help them. My job is very relationship driven."

In addition to making connections, the EDC has supported and partnered with Emerging Prairie to develop programs targeted to entrepreneurs and the startup community. "*Startup Weekend was a spark for us, 1 Million Cups was putting gasoline on it,*" he said.

Other Emerging Prairie-driven initiatives include the networking event Startup Drinks, a coworking space and monthly e-commerce and drone-related events that have also led to the creation of annual conferences for those sectors.

"Emerging Prairie is now a 501(c)(3). We talked about combining, about making them part of the EDC. But this way they can act as their own grassroots organization, with the sole focus on engaging and celebrating the startup scene. They can act more entrepreneurial by being more agile in their ideas and actions."

And how has this infrastructure helped entrepreneurs?

"There was this startup, Botlink, who presented at 1MC. They weren't even sure if they wanted to do it. Emerging Prairie did a story on them and the next thing you know, people in Europe were calling them, venture capitalists were calling them.

"Another woman had a couple of businesses and was burned out. She had told herself she'd give the business another couple of weeks and then she'd close it. She came to 1MC and was so energized she told herself, 'I'm going to keep doing this.' It was a way of introducing her into the community. Now she has a support system, she's started another business, she's on the board for Emerging Prairie. For her it was a life changing moment."

Machacek said he hears those kinds of stories all the time. And it's not just entrepreneurs who benefit.

"We're trying to get more people to think, 'I can do this and I want to do it in Fargo.' There's a lot of community pride. It's building confidence in entrepreneurs. It's the spirit."

Mobilizing the Network

The Cork (Ireland) Innovates Partnership has provided a framework to bring together agencies and multi-level ideas to drive Cork's economic ecosystem since 2012. This is achieved by leading the way for regional stakeholders including local government, state agencies, educational institutions, business support organizations, entrepreneurs and the extended Cork business community to engage in a collaborative and complementary manner.

Reigniting the passion for entrepreneurship

Kathy Wyatt, the director of the Louisiana Tech University Technology Business Development Center, has been working with entrepreneurs for years. She's a firm believer in making the most of what's in the community.

"We are strong believers in understanding the asset base and then figuring out how you build upon and leverage those opportunities. We try to focus on those things that are great strengths and resources."

One of the "hidden" resources they began tapping into were the successful entrepreneurs and executives in the community.

"We thought it would be neat to invite successful entrepreneurs to be participants with us in training and networking activities. We did it in a guest panel type format. We knew they had things to contribute but they were too busy, they had no time to prepare a lecture or a presentation. All were willing and eager to help grow entrepreneurs.

"In doing this we were able to gain access to this tremendous wealth of resources and connect them with aspiring entrepreneurs so the young founders could gain knowledge and get connected to these experienced folks. It's proven to be helpful to the nascent entrepreneurs for obvious reasons.

"What we did not expect is that the executives would often become inspired and amazed at what they saw. They came to our meeting and renewed their vows to entrepreneurship. They realized that they were no longer that enthused, eager and excited as they once were, and so far removed that they had forgotten what it was like to be really in love with their business and their business idea. We reignited a passion for entrepreneurship in the hearts of these business executives.

"It's pretty cool."

In 2010 Cork City and County Councils took the groundbreaking step of creating the Economic Development Fund, dedicated to the support of enterprise at a regional level. This regional economic development fund has supported the creation and expansion of sustainable enterprises and support initiatives across the micro and small/medium enterprise sectors of the economy within the Cork region. One of these initiatives is The Cork Innovates Partnership.

The ambition of the Partnership is to drive the entrepreneurial culture throughout the region. By adopting a collaborative approach and taking a balanced view on the promotion of entrepreneurship across all industry sectors, Cork Innovates pioneers a regionally unique collaborative approach to entrepreneurship.

The Partnership acted as the local host and tertiary partner when Startup Ireland secured the rights to host the Startup Nations Summit in Ireland in 2016, bringing the event to Europe for the first time. The Startup Nations Summit is a gathering of startup community leaders and policymakers.

Siobhan Finn, executive director of Cork Innovates, tells the story. *"With the resources and support of a partner-driven network, Cork was able to maximize the engagement and mobilize resources at a local level."*

Simply winning the opportunity to host the event was a measure of the network's strength. What happened at the summit were also measures of success.

"A key legacy of the weekend of activity is the number of new relationships and collaborations – local, national and international – that have developed and that should lead to driving economic success for individuals, for companies and for the region.

"What did the summit mean for Cork Innovates and our individual partners? There was increased international recognition, our reputation among our peers was enhanced, we had opportunities to engage with international colleagues, we contributed to the local economy and we brought more exposure to Ireland and Cork as areas of academic excellence as well as a tourist destination.

"We were the only region with a structure in place that wove together the resources to make it happen."

Hosting the summit yielded other results. *"It is impossible to sum up the combination of experiences, encounters and challenges in the 12 months surrounding the summit preparation and delivery, but what I do know with certainly is that the summit was good for Ireland and great for Cork. It put Cork on the map. That's the challenge every second city has. It put Cork on an international stage, with international influence and reach.*

"We generated 40 newspaper articles, 90 online articles, got 12 million impressions with our social media hashtags. The value of that exposure was equal to €425,000 and a reach of almost 5 million people."

The connected network of entrepreneurs, support organizations, government and education provided the foundation upon which Cork is now building a bright future for their entrepreneurs and innovators.

Leadership tip:

The secret sauce to making a network work is collaboration. But the real magic is the leadership it takes to pull people together, stand in the background and let others claim the spotlight. You are going to have to bite your tongue a thousand times ... or maybe a hundred thousand times. We call it "speaking with a short tongue."

When you are in the business of building entrepreneurial infrastructure, there are a lot of things that are going to happen that you can't take credit for. You have to look at that as the best kind of endorsement, when people are so passionate they take all that support you gave them and do good things and then take the credit.

Sometimes it means not reacting, staying focused on the long-term vision. Don't trip over the small stones so you can't make the whole journey.

Almost everything you do is based on relationships and making the other person look good. You have to be a cheerleader for everybody.

Once some of your resource providers sink their teeth into a gap and band together to solve it, you'll be amazed at the ways your entrepreneurial community can grow. Keep reminding people of the end goal, and how their solution works toward that goal.

5. EMPOWER

"Entrepreneurship is about designing the future. We need to make connections and bring the ecosystem together."

-Jeff Hoffman, founder of PriceLine

Identifying assets is one thing. Building an entrepreneurial community is another.

Just as a single program doesn't make an entrepreneurial ecosystem, having an online list of available resources does not make an entrepreneurial infrastructure. A network becomes effective when it listens, engages, responds and collaborates to solve problems and fill gaps within the entrepreneurial infrastructure. Connecting and activating a resource network causes strategic and dynamic change the community.

In the process of talking to Resource Partners and entrepreneurs, you'll start to hear some emerging themes about strengths and gaps. Go after the gaps with all your strength: they hold your best opportunities.

We talk about working in the white space. The gaps define the white space, where the community has unmet needs. Here's where you'll find no competition and a chance to do something of real value for your entrepreneurs and business owners.

The beauty of this work is that funders look for a strong problem statement and collaboration among groups to fill gaps. You will have the information you need to seek additional funding for your programs.

Step by Step: Empowering the Network

1. Understand your entrepreneurial community
2. Identify the gaps
3. Empower the champion(s) to find a workable solution for the gap
4. Fund the network
5. Implement, adjust and measure the results

You have to have a network, a foundation, on which to build these kinds of innovative solutions. By identifying and connecting resources, you will begin to develop a deep understanding of your entrepreneurial community. You'll start to see what's going on beneath the surface, what's really working well and what needs are not being met.

In Kansas City, learning about the entrepreneurial community allowed us to debunk some myths. For instance, when we first started KCSourceLink, there was some concern among entrepreneurs as to the quality of the support resource services. We collected satisfaction data for every referral we made and discovered that as we learned more about the resources, and made better referrals, satisfaction levels went up. In 2016 entrepreneurs reported 99.2 percent satisfaction with the referrals that KCSourceLink made.

We also heard investors tell us there were no good deals, and entrepreneurs told us there was no money for early-stage companies. KCSourceLink did a deep dive into data about who was getting funding from whom and discovered that while both sides were a little bit right, there was significant mismatching between investors and entrepreneurs, on both the debt and equity sides. Entrepreneurs were asking the wrong sources for the wrong amount of money at the wrong time. There was little connectivity among investors themselves, and little with the entrepreneurs. Again, learning in more detail what the investors and loan programs were looking for, and communicating that more clearly to the entrepreneurs led to better matches and more deals/loans.

In addition to learning about the community, connecting resources enables you to build a distribution network for future initiatives. NetWork Kansas has discovered that this is one of the most valuable assets they've created. When Kansas received its State Small Business Credit Initiative funds from the U.S. Treasury as part of the Small Business Jobs Act of 2010, the state turned to NetWork Kansas to deploy the funds. Because NetWork Kansas had a strong statewide network of partners, they were able to get the funds invested more quickly and more effectively than most states, earning them kudos from the U.S. Treasury.

Identify the Gaps

How do you figure out gaps in the market? In addition to developing processes to gather feedback from resource partners and entrepreneurs through focus groups and discussions, SourceLink also developed the Biz-Trakker® decision management system to aid in making data-driven decisions about what challenges to tackle in a community. (More about Biz-Trakker in Chapter 6.)

It is easier to attract funders by explaining how you'll fill gaps in the entrepreneurial ecosystem than it is to create a new program from scratch and with scant data. Programs that fill gaps are data-driven, defensible and sustainable. They have the capacity to live on and deliver impact.

Empower the Community Champion

Once you have a clear, well defined gap, it's time to rally resources to solve the problem. For the most part, people and organizations will opt in to projects that align with their organizations' mission or their own passions.

How do you begin? Work with the willing. Some other folks are going to see the gap as clearly as you do, and will want to get involved. Let them. Lead them. You don't have to, and you don't want to, do all of this alone. Meg Wheatley, in her work on creating healthy communities, says, "People support what they create." In our experience it's absolutely true. If people are engaged in the development of programming to fill gaps, they have ownership, a stake in that initiative's continuing sustainability and success.

The key is communicating the gap and then seeing who steps up. Later in this chapter we'll talk about several instances of filling gaps. The common denominator is that champions arose in each instance; we didn't have to twist arms to get people involved.

Implement, Adjust and Measure

Once your champion or champions have figured out a workable solution, it's time to implement. Chances are the solution/program/initiative will not be perfect right out of the gate. To paraphrase Helmuth Von Moltke, German military strategist, "No plan survives contact with the enemy."

The entrepreneurs will tell you if you are on the right track. You'll probably have to tweak a few things, maybe pivot a time or two. You have to be entrepreneurial about growing entrepreneurship. The most important thing you can do is measure to ensure you are getting the impact you desire and actually filling the gap you've identified.

We've seen these steps play out over and over in the 15 years we've been working with KCSourceLink.

Gap 1: Marketing startup classes

When KCSourceLink first started, there were nearly a dozen different organizations offering a basic "How to Start a Business" class. Not surprisingly, everyone was having trouble filling the classes. KCSourceLink pulled together a meeting of those organizations to start a conversation about marketing startup classes.

There was no preconceived notion about how this gap would be solved. No hidden agenda. The result was surprising. Most of the organizations decided to quit offering a startup class, and start referring clients to the three that were still going to operate. Turns out those organizations felt they could provide more benefit to clients a bit beyond the startup stage. The remaining organizations decided to collaborate on marketing, and develop a bookmark that they distributed through the libraries listing all the starting-a-business classes.

Gap 2: Microlending returns to Kansas City

When Kansas City's primary microloan program closed in 2009, it created a huge void for early-stage entrepreneurs. The door had barely closed on the old program when a concerned group, initiated by KCSourceLink, began talking about how to fill the gap.

The Women's Employment Network, the Women's Business Center, the University of Missouri–Kansas City Small Business and Technology Development Center, the Johnson County Community College Small Business Development Center, the Federal Reserve Bank, the Small Business Administration and the Federal Deposit Insurance Corp. – all these organizations came to the table, joined by another resource, St. Louis-based Justine PETERSEN.

The KC Regional Microloan Program emerged from those meetings. The program serves seven counties with loans of less than $50,000. Participating companies receive counseling on how to improve credit scores and put together solid business plans.

Gap 3: Bringing innovation into the marketplace

Institutions of higher education have struggled to move research innovations to market. The most successful have been those with the greatest amount of federal funding. The Kansas City region doesn't have the likes of MIT or Stanford, so in 2009 a group of schools came together to explore how to maximize the value of research in local university laboratories by getting it into the hands of entrepreneurs who could commercialize it.

Led by the University of Missouri–Kansas City Innovation Center, a National Science Foundation *Partnership for Innovation* grant created the Whiteboard2Boardroom program as a partnership between four regional schools – UMKC, University of Kansas, Johnson County Community College and William Jewell College.

The W2B team successfully developed a simple and effective method to "pull" technologies from research institutions. The approach consists of (a) identifying promising new technologies, (b) "matching" those innovations to entrepreneurs and established companies with the ability to commercialize them, and (c) providing connections to the right community resources that support business startup and development.

This successful collaboration grew from the four founding institutions to now include 21 research organizations across our bistate region. It has helped facilitate 29 new startups around technologies and created nearly 100 new jobs. One of the first companies to be based on an innovation from an affiliated university, Zoloz, recently sold for $100+ million.

Gap 4: Proof-of-concept funding

The success with the Whiteboard2Boardroom program revealed another gap: the lack of proof-of-concept funds. If an entrepreneur did not have the personal funds to build out a prototype, the innovations coming out of W2B would not move forward.

Another collaboration emerged: this time among private companies, universities, entrepreneurial support organizations and government agencies across a two-state region. Launched in February 2013 with a

U.S. Commerce Department i6 challenge grant, Digital Sandbox KC has become a highly successful proof-of-concept program that has worked with more than 300 entrepreneurs and early-stage companies across the metro area.

Digital Sandbox KC provides proof-of-concept resources including market validation, prototyping and beta-testing support for development of digital technologies within new and existing businesses. To date the program has created 34 new companies, 480+ new jobs and the companies have raised more than $38 million in follow-on funding.

These particular programs got started in Kansas City, but they could happen anywhere, because communities across the United States grapple with the same issues: how do we best serve our entrepreneurs' needs, how do we build a pipeline of innovations and how do we fund early, early stage ideas.

Other communities have used a similar "gap-filling" strategy to address issues facing their entrepreneurs.

Gap 5: Visibility for entrepreneurs

Vanessa Wagner works as the small business and entrepreneurship manager for the Loudoun County Department of Economic Development.

"My role is unique. I'm not recruiting businesses. I'm here to support existing small business and to build the ecosystem that enables them to grow."

When Wagner joined the department, she saw a gap between the visibility of large corporations versus small firms.

"A lot of times there's not a face for a small business owner unless it's a retail operation."

Her solution: a campaign called "Small Business, Big Success" that launched in November 2015.

"The mission or goal was to highlight different entrepreneurs in the community representing our important clusters but also those you wouldn't easily recognize, like government consultants. Most people think of small business as a bakery, retail.

"Through the campaign we were able to highlight 12 different businesses. We also asked

each business owner which resources they used to grow or start. That was important because the other gap was that entrepreneurs or potential entrepreneurs didn't know about community resources."

The campaign featured 12 videos that were posted on social media and the Loudoun Economic Development website. The companies ranged from biotechnology to wealth management to brewing.

"The videos created awareness of successful small businesses and also the resources that helped them reach that success." (See videos at www.loudounsmallbiz.org).

"We got to meet one-on-one with the businesses, learn things we didn't know and provide additional assistance if it was needed."

The result: more awareness for Loudoun County entrepreneurs.

"Looking back, meeting Vanessa (Wagner from Loudoun County) and engaging in the entrepreneurial meetups that Loudoun's Economic Development group sponsored was what led to our initial growth. Whether it is aviation related or networking related, they always have and still come through for me. Most importantly it's great to see that they see Loudoun County has the potential to be known for other industries beyond data centers and are actively trying to foster an environment that can make that happen."

-Ravi Gangele, founder, Raven
Loudoun County, Virginia

Gap 6: Programming for women

Ann Marie Wallace is very proud of the online training programs developed to assist women entrepreneurs by the Salt Lake Chamber Women's Business Center, where she is executive director.

The WBC conducted focus groups to gather feedback from women about the types of services needed and user experience with the online format. The focus groups revealed a gap in services designed for women entrepreneurs and ideas on how to fill that gap.

Based on the feedback, WBC initiated their online training portal that provides training by topic and a 15-module video course called "Build Your Dream Company."

One success story involved Marian Rivkind. Rivkind fondly remembered a Russian holiday tradition of gifting chocolate foil-wrapped tree ornaments and decided to start a business, Yolka Chocolates, selling elegant chocolate Christmas tree ornaments and chocolate-covered matzoth.

WBC helped Rivkind write her business plan. It took her a year to secure funding from a microlender, with her business plan playing a key part in that process. Rivkind has been featured in *Oprah Magazine* and is distributing her product online through various outlets.

Gap 7: A convening point for entrepreneurs

Norris Krueger, a recovering tech entrepreneur and research Ph.D. in entrepreneurship, has been immersed in the tech scene in Idaho, especially Boise. A new coworking space there provides an example of how committed entrepreneurs can make something special happen to fill a gap.

"Trailhead (in Boise) is a true coworking space. People here are building companies and doing creative things. Trailhead was a white elephant building in a semitrendy neighborhood. The city and the civic development company that handles downtown wanted to get involved, and they figured out a way to give a very favorable lease to the team of entrepreneurs who wanted to make this happen.

"They were hoping to get a couple hundred members. They did 100 in less than a year, and at age two, they're at about 400. It's exploded.

"They've been neutral turf for a number of activities. We do 1 Million Cups here. We do Startup Grind events here. Different classes, both internal and external. Mentoring and office hours. It's kind of cool, but also very organic and entrepreneur-led. Trailhead's success derives from that and not being hostage to institutional players. If one of my friends who are luminaries in entrepreneurship – like Kauffman (Foundation) or SourceLink – came to town, THIS is the only place to host them.

"There's this great energy here that you don't find in every incubator or accelerator – a lot of random conversation, ideas that will come out and move forward eventually."

Trailhead got started because a group of serial entrepreneurs wanted to make it happen.

"Two had founded successful companies here, the third one had been involved in a venture and was an exec in Silicon Valley. The fourth one has been active behind the scenes. He was a partner in KPMG, with ventures on the side. He started asking, 'How do we move the city and downtown area forward.' Quite the visionary … all of them, really.

"They were frustrated that the energy around entrepreneurship wasn't focused. They wanted to create that convening point, that rallying point.

"This is the two-year anniversary of Trailhead. New management is coming in, it will be interesting to see what happens. Trailhead has become a brand name, people tend to think of it positively. A year from now the story may be very different. I'm hoping it will be even better."

It's Not about You

At NetWork Kansas, CEO Steve Radley and Vice President Erik Pedersen brought an entrepreneurial outlook to the challenge of bolstering entrepreneurship across the state of Kansas. Not content to simply run a statewide resource hotline and loan program, Radley and Pedersen conceived the idea of E-Communities.

"We did 18 town hall meetings, which is really where the idea of E-Communities came from. The buzz word was empower – empower people, empower communities. We knew if we didn't do something different, it would be a transaction. Yes, it would help that one entrepreneur, but it wouldn't change the system. We felt like if we were really going to empower people, we had to put our assets on the line."

An E-Community is a partnership that allows a town, a cluster of towns, or an entire county to raise seed money for local entrepreneurs through donations from individuals or businesses within the community. The E-Community Partnership has grown from six communities in 2007 to 55 in 2016. During the first nine years of the E-Community partnership, more than $9.7 million has been loaned to more than 360 businesses, leveraging $47 million of additional capital.

"We decided to take half of our assets and dedicate them to communities where we would not be making the decision. If we were going to make an impact, it wasn't going to be us, it was going to be them."

Radley learned early, especially in western Kansas, that relationships were the most important thing.

"You cannot come in and out of communities. It will not work. You have to be part of them or you're not going to be successful. Even if you have great ideas, you have no credibility. And they are the ones who are going to have to do the work.

"It's one thing to say we want to help you. It's another thing to say we want to empower you, be with you. You'll make the decisions. You'll set up the review board. We'll provide the assets.

"For us, it was like 'This could be something different. This could be something that could make a long term impact.' And we could set up sustainable assets. If you make good loans, you get to make more loans. You have to think about how we can sustain it in the long term. For us, that's why the loan money was important."

That's not how most state-run programs work.

"Quite frankly, the culture of this type of work is that there are too many strings, too much telling the community how something must be done. Most of our best ideas have emerged out of the E-Communities."

NetWork Kansas still runs a statewide loan program as well as the E-Communities program. *"We thought they (the E-Community teams) would make better decisions about loans. And they did. They know the entrepreneur, they know what's going on. Theirs is a 9 percent default rate. Statewide is closer to the 15 percent range."*

NetWork Kansas has not only built a series of supportive entrepreneurial communities, they've developed a connected distribution network.

"Now we have scale. When we do something, we can get it out to a huge group. Now we have a funnel. When we get assets we can funnel them across a much bigger area than most programs because we have point-to-point distribution.

"If you're going to do this work, you have to be super intentional. It's hard to build that (entrepreneurial) culture from outside the community. The only thing you can do is build the leadership, infuse the assets into the community, and then let them build the culture."

Lessons in Empowerment

Tom Lyons, currently the director of the Michigan State University Product Center, has spent a career studying and encouraging entrepreneurs. He shares some lessons about what works and why.

How do communities get engaged in entrepreneurship?

"How does entrepreneurship come to the fore and become important? Usually it involves some kind of thought leaders, and they can come from anywhere, from inside the community or outside."

Lyons cited the example of the work done by the Center for Rural Entrepreneurship, an organization that helps communities think about what helps entrepreneurs in rural communities.

"They can start at the top and get community leaders engaged. Then they (the community leaders) can help it move forward."

Lyons mentioned other catalysts for a community deciding to support entrepreneurship.

"People observe their neighbors and want what they have. That causes some communities to get engaged. I don't think we should underestimate the power of the written word, blog posts, presentations … these are all ways that ideas spread."

Engaging a community is not a quick process.

"In my own experience, when we were approaching folks in the Advantage Valley region (of Appalachia), I probably went to that region at least seven times to make presentations. It wasn't that I was presenting anything that different. Slowly but surely things started to catch on … Often it takes several times for people to hear things before they absorb them and are moved to do something about them."

Who takes the lead?

"I think different people in different organizations can, depending on the community. I've seen several cases where funders, like community foundations, take the lead by putting money behind it and people follow. Sometimes it's government. In Buenos Aires, it started because the government wanted to do something. But they knew that if they did it alone, nothing would happen. So they turned the leadership over to the entrepreneurs to make it happen. Sometimes universities take the lead.

"At the Michigan State University Product Center, the whole goal is to help entrepreneurs who want to start a business in the food industry. We try to put resources together for them. We have innovation counselors who give advice and make referrals. We have campus staff who can help with labeling, food safety, consumer testing and the like."

Lyons said this kind of engagement is written into the DNA of land grant universities.

"The whole land grant university system was built to be accountable to the communities

that they serve. With a land grant university, we generate new knowledge, but it's not helpful until you get it out to people who need it. We help people actualize it. It's engagement, it's more than reaching out, it's really getting involved with the community.

"It's an interesting debate, about whether entrepreneurs should take the lead or not. You need more than just the entrepreneurs. Entrepreneurs can pick it up once it gets going."

How do you get people to the table?

"First of all, as is the case with any change agenda, you have to have a champion. It can be an organization, an individual, a loose collection of individuals. I've seen it all ways. Outside conveners, like the Center for Rural Entrepreneurship, have had a lot of success in helping communities make entrepreneurs out of community leaders … showing them how to be asset based vs. focused on a problem … ultimately putting them in a position where they can create their own ecosystem.

"One of the big carrots is always money. If someone with money wants to see something happen, you can get a lot of people in line. That may not be the best way to be sustainable. You want people doing it because it's the right thing or they like the results of what they are doing."

And when they are at the table, what do you do?

"I was involved in an interesting effort. One city government was concerned because they had been making investments in entrepreneurial support organizations but they were seeing a lot of dysfunction, people not working together, outcomes not up to expectations. I did a deep dive into what everyone was doing … they thought they were in competition but they were not. The whole idea was to put the puzzle together differently so that it fit, bringing together ESOs (entrepreneurial support organizations) and getting them past holding their cards close to the vest and jointly solving problems.

"You have to have facilitated conversations by a neutral third party. You get everyone together. It's this disparate group looking suspiciously at each other, seeing each other as competitors. They don't want to be there. Then the facilitator begins to work on them, engage them, they begin to start realizing that they are not in competition, they are not the enemy, they care about what happens in this community. After a couple of months what used to be a frigid situation has now turned into a situation where people are hugging and asking about each other's families. It's a totally different dynamic.

"You get them to consider the challenges, how can we address these. They come up with

fantastic solutions and work to make them happen. You get people to see that they are on a team, make it possible for them to work together, and build trust. And it takes time. If you don't have the time, you might as well walk away.

"One of the biggest things that happens is that you are giving them a lingua franca. They all come from their silos, they have their own jargon, they live in their own world, they don't always understand each other. If you give them a common language, they can begin to work together."

Leadership tip:

If you want to do something, you just have to show up. That's important. Go where people are and listen to what they say and be part of the whole fabric. You don't lead by having a title or a position. You lead by jumping in and getting things rolling.

You want to hand everyone who meets with you something that makes their life a little better … an idea, a connection … and you keep doing that.

Building an entrepreneurial infrastructure involves identifying, connecting and empowering the resources in your community. Then you need to measure progress and impact. Measurement depends entirely on what you are trying to achieve. And for most communities, it's more jobs, more startups, sales increases and debt/equity infusion. People track those numbers and then benchmark them against other places.

6. MEASURE WHAT MATTERS

"Data, data, data. I can't make bricks without clay!"
-Sir Arthur Conan Doyle, author

"In God we trust, all others must bring data."
-W. Edwards Deming, father of modern quality management

"The goal is to turn data into information, and information into insight."
-Carly Fiorina, former CEO, Hewlett-Packard

At SourceLink we believe that you can effectively build a better support structure for your entrepreneurs by identifying your assets and connecting them together. You must connect your assets to the entrepreneurs in the region as well. By using data to identify gaps and collaborating to fill those gaps, you will empower the ecosystem. We also believe that you can measure the development and impact of the system over time by understanding those gaps, devising plans to fill them and using metrics to measure progress.

Measurement depends entirely on what you are trying to achieve. And for most communities, it's more jobs, more startups, sales increases and debt/ equity infusion. People track those numbers and then benchmark them against other places.

The problem with benchmarking with other places is that you need to use data that can be collected everywhere. That may mean that you are only seeing a macro view.

What matters most is what your community is trying to accomplish, not how it compares to another community. Understanding your community, the needs and the gaps, will help you determine what metrics matter.

Step by Step: Measuring What Matters

1. Figure out the end game; what's the outcome/goal/objective
2. Find the right data
3. If the right data is unavailable, develop a system to collect it
4. Report to the community

Begin with the End in Mind

One of author and educator Stephen Covey's famous habits of highly effective people is to begin with the end in mind. This is particularly important when it comes to metrics. If you don't know what you want to achieve, no amount of data will help you.

Hundreds of books have been written on goal setting. It doesn't have to be complicated. You've started with a clear gap to be filled, a problem to be solved. Knowing the resources available and how entrepreneurs interact with the resources that are available to them can demonstrate gaps. How far do people reach for resources and how many reach out to the same ones? What's missing?

Picture the future. What would it look like if you fill the gap or solve the problem? What would there be more of? Less of? That should give you a pretty good idea of what you should try to measure.

Sometimes it's appropriate to measure activity as well as outcomes. Creating collaborations that measure key information across organizations can help you find out what is happening in the community. Whiteboard2Boardroom, a collaboration among 23 research organizations in the Kansas City region, consolidates available early-stage technologies into one place and tracks projects that are moving them to commercialization. The program allows Kansas City to go beyond the typical measure of patent activity to measure what innovations are actually moving toward business startup, demonstrating a true pipeline of innovation.

When you are building an entrepreneurial infrastructure, you can't measure everything at the beginning. The best early measures may **not** be jobs, sales and debt/equity infusion. Early on, it might be better to measure how well different parts of the system are working together: who is connecting, how are they connecting and where are they connecting?

Collect Your Own Data

When all else fails, you may have to collect your own data. On the plus side, you'll have control of what you collect from whom and when. On the minus side, it's expensive and time consuming to do data collection.

Biz-Trakker® was originally built to collect information that was not available from any other source. The software collects a variety of data points on those who come to KCSourceLink for assistance: demographics, needs, stage of business and more. By mining that data, we are able to see trends in what kinds of businesses are opening; what kind of help is most requested (and what people need that is missing); and how that information compares based on gender, ethnicity, race and geography.

A key benefit of Biz-Trakker is that it enables the organization to own the contacts and connections, rather than one individual. It also addresses the age-old problem of "I have that list right here in my head," which works fine until the list gets too long or your brain gets too full.

In Kansas City, we use Biz-Trakker to connect together the underlying people involved in the entrepreneurial infrastructure. That framework allows us to make better connections between entrepreneurs and a variety of resource people and helps us understand the entire system.

We are also able to survey clients using Biz-Trakker. KCSourceLink instituted an annual survey about 10 years ago, and has been asking a set of core questions each year. This allows us to look at how things have changed over time, both in overall trends and in individual outcomes for clients. Questions in the annual survey cover topics such as change in revenue, change in number of employees, sources of financing and connections (Figures 7 and 8).

Read All about It

Data can be a powerful motivator when positioned appropriately and shared with the right people. Yearly reports can help the community see progress and inspire continued action. Wrapping real numbers around a problem can help people see the depth of an issue and encourage action.

We Create KC℠ is an annual report to the Kansas City community on the status of entrepreneurship. The report features stories of entrepreneurs as well as the data on the six imperatives for making Kansas City America's most entrepreneurial city – one of five big goals set forth by the Greater Kansas City Chamber of Commerce. The report is typically launched with a public event, is mailed to community leaders and is distributed through entrepreneurial support organizations that are part of the KCSourceLink

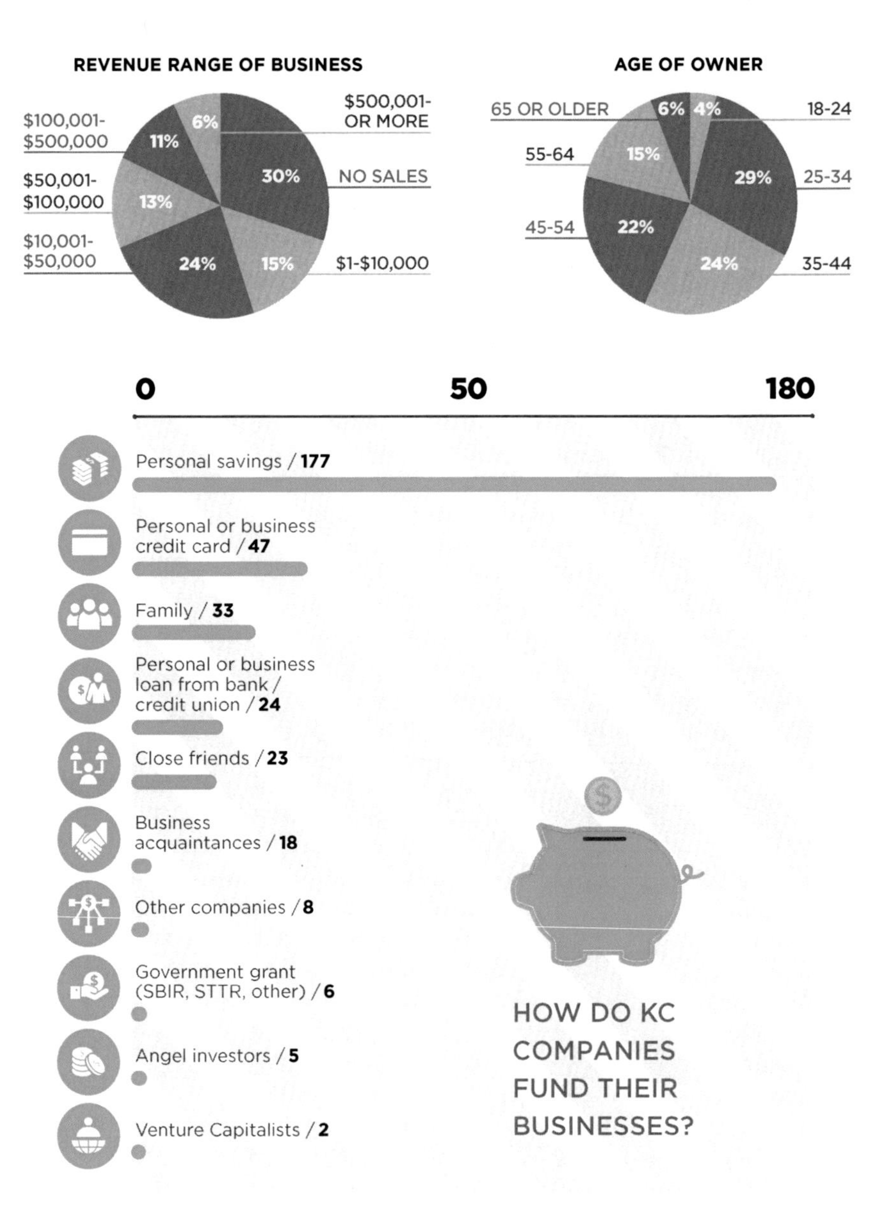

Figures 7 and 8: Examples of KCSourceLink annual survey results

network. The report not only gives the Kansas City community a year-to-year picture of what's happening in entrepreneurship, it also tells the KC story around the country (wecreatekc.com).

We Create Capital℠ 2015 followed on the heels of the first We Create KC report, but with a different objective. The We Create Capital report was intended to educate the community about significant gaps in the capital continuum for early-stage companies. The report looked at levels of debt, grant and equity funding, and provided a roadmap for improving the status quo.

The community embraced the report more than anyone expected. Within a few years of its publication, Kansas City saw improvement in the pools of capital available to entrepreneurs. The report was widely noted as a catalyst for several individuals and organizations to engage.

A Hierarchy of Measures

We've developed a hierarchy of metrics that can be used all along the path as a community develops its network of support for entrepreneurs. The measures coincide with the steps in creating an entrepreneurial infrastructure.

Identify: Measuring an emerging network

At the earliest stage of building entrepreneurial infrastructure, the goal is simply to inventory the entrepreneurship support resources already present and active in the community. At this stage, success can be measured by how many resources are willing to participate in a collaborative effort. Metrics might include:

- Number of network partners
- Number of network partner meetings
- Number of entrepreneurial events listed on a central calendar

The number of resources participating to support entrepreneurs; number of events and attendance at those events; and the reach of the network through social media channels can serve as early measurements of an entrepreneurial infrastructure.

Connect: Measuring an active network

As partners begin to interact and know each other and promotion begins to draw people to a central hub, the focus shifts to usage of network services. Accessibility and visibility metrics begin to "count." Depending on what components you've implemented in your community (website, hotline), the following metrics might apply:

Network Access

(How many entrepreneurs are using the resources in your entrepreneurial infrastructure?)

- Web sessions
- Hotline calls
- Searches for assistance

Network Strength

(How much participation do you see from entrepreneurial support organizations?)

- Partners
- Calendar events
- Satisfaction survey results

Network Reach

(How visible is the entrepreneurial infrastructure? (Figure 9)*)*

- Friends and Followers
- Sources of traffic

Figure 9: Example of social metric reporting

Empower: Measuring collaboration and network leverage

A network becomes more effective as it engages, listens, responds and collaborates to solve problems and fill gaps within the entrepreneurial ecosystem. Programs that fill gaps can be measured in terms of:

- Gap reports
- Entrepreneurial activity snapshots
- Jobs
- Startups
- Revenues
- Debt/equity infusion
- Specific program results

Building Your Dashboard

Dashboards are a hot topic in the discussion of how to track progress for companies, organizations and projects. A dashboard is a way of tracking key performance indicators and other data points (Figures 10 and 11).

Of course, you can't build a dashboard until you know what you want to measure. In every community where SourceLink has worked, the answer has been different. Industries are different, resources are different, communication channels are different, power bases are different.

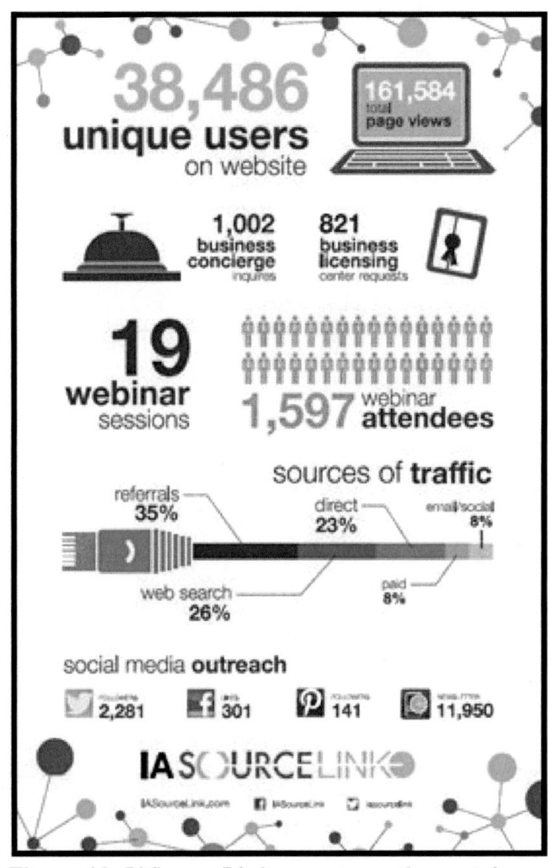

Figure 10: IASourceLink reports on the metrics of its active network

Once you are clear about what you want to measure, the next step is to find data that will give you an accurate and timely picture. It is crucial that your data be accurate, timely, relatively easy/ inexpensive to access, and available on a regular basis. If you are

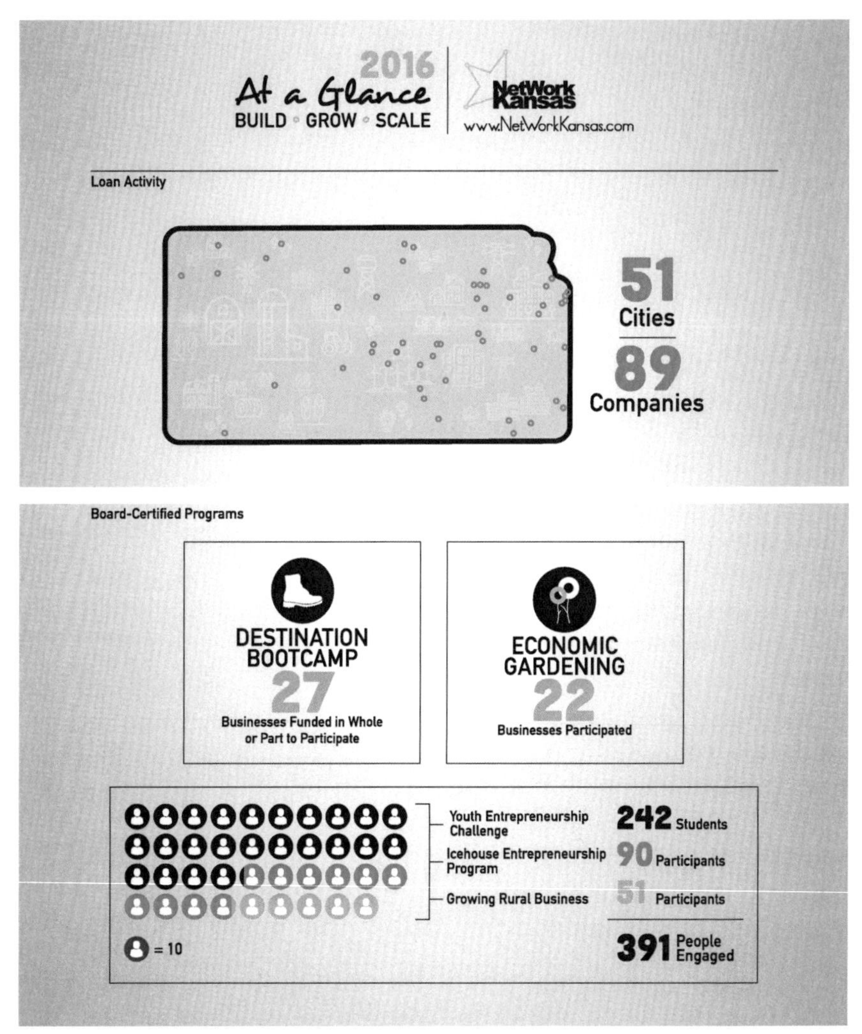

Figure 11: NetWork Kansas shares the impact of collaborative programs

going to compare results year over year, you need to be able to have a replicable process with a consistent data set. You'll start with the ideal, and then as reality crashes in you'll figure out what's feasible.

When the Greater Kansas City Chamber of Commerce set a goal to make Kansas City America's most entrepreneurial city, one of the first things KCSourceLink did was to work with others in the community to determine how that would be measured and what data could be used.

In this case, it came down to six imperatives: an entrepreneurial infrastructure to support entrepreneurs; an idea pipeline to cultivate and support ideas; a talent pool to feed new startups and advance new ideas; financing and capital to help companies accelerate; national microphone and spotlight to tell and share stories; and commitment from corporations to mentor, lead and engage.

For each of the six imperatives we developed key metrics. Some were pretty easy to define. For infrastructure, it was the number of partners participating in the KCSourceLink network. For innovation pipeline, it was the number and type of innovations coming through the Whiteboard2Boardroom program.

For a few, it was a lot easier to figure out the metric than to find the data. For the talent pool, we started by looking at current openings in tech jobs in the Kansas City metro area, along with the graduate supply in STEM (Science, Technology, Engineering and Math) fields. We were able to pull that from a database accessible to one of our partners. The next year, the dataset was no longer accessible, so we had to search for a more public set of information. We settled on STEM job postings and job hires, available from a public source.

Capital was another area that sent us down a lot of blind alleys. We must have sorted through a dozen or more options before settling on the data that we collect today. In order to meet the criteria of inexpensive we partner with another organization to gain access to a proprietary database that captures equity investments.

Jobs created also presented some challenges. Most of the publicly available data on job creation lags a few years. We wanted something more timely. We learned that a group in Colorado worked through the governor's office to access information from the Quarterly Census of Employment and Wages. It took about two years of negotiation, but we were finally able to get the same information for Missouri and Kansas. That data allows us to create "hot spot" charts of firms hiring their first employees (Figure 12).

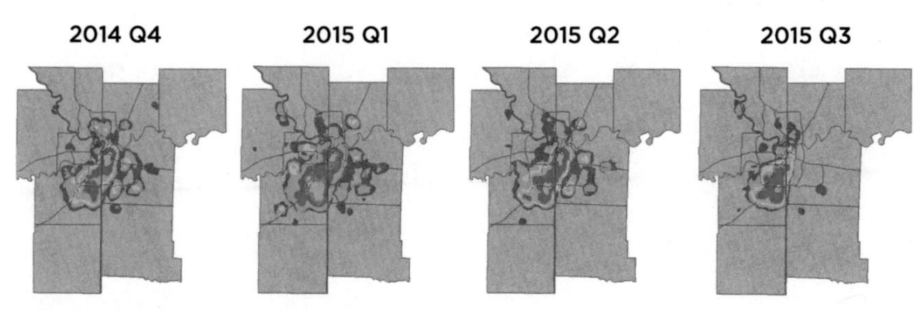

Figure 12: Entrepreneurial density in the Kansas City metro area

Engaging and changing the system requires understanding your community at a deep level. What needs to change? How does it need to change? Which needle do you want to move? It's not so much how you compare to other communities, but what would make your community better.

In Kansas City we decided to tackle the issue of capital for early-stage entrepreneurs. We wanted to increase the number of early-stage companies that obtain equity financing and the amount of capital available to those companies. While it's interesting to know how our share of equity investment compares with peer cities, it's more important to see if the number of equity deals is increasing or decreasing year over year, and if the pool of investment is changing.

The dashboard for the KCSourceLink capital project encompasses charts like those found in Figures 13 and 14 below.

Measure what matters

Determine where you are in the process of developing your entrepreneurial infrastructure and track the metrics that match that stage. Be consistent with how you collect data and what data sources you use, so that you are comparing apples to apples. And don't worry so much about what other communities are doing. Track progress from where you were to where you are. That information can rally your community and help drive it to where you want to be tomorrow.

Beyond Jobs: Measuring a Network

Siobhan Finn, with The Cork Innovates Partnership, brings together entrepreneurs, organizations, government and education under one brand to promote the Cork, Ireland story. From the earliest days, they've focused on metrics and key performance indicators.

The Cork Innovates Partnership has always focused on supporting and fueling the entrepreneurial reputation of the region. The Partnership provides communication and marketing supports for stakeholders, according to each individual partner member's vision, mission and objectives.

The initiative has worked with the enterprise development system in Cork to make it the best location in Ireland to start a business. This has been achieved by working with regional stakeholders such as local government, state agencies, educational institutions, business support organizations, entrepreneurs and the extended Cork business community, in a collaborative and complementary manner, to promote the Cork story.

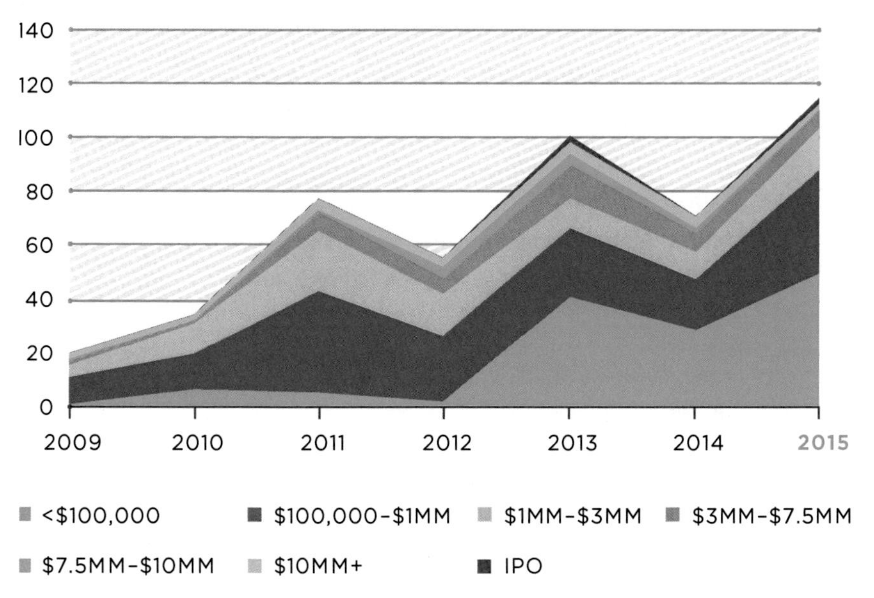

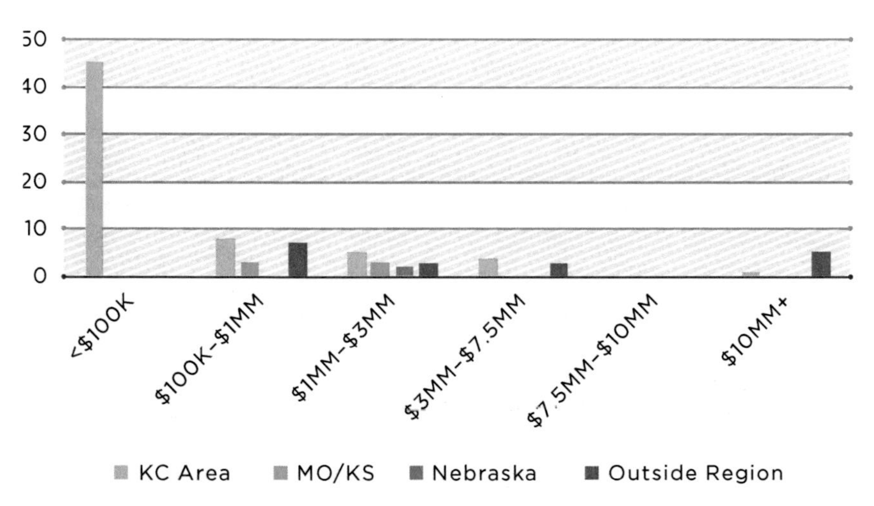

Figures 13 and 14: Examples of KCSourceLink capital project dashboard components

"It takes about five to eight years to get to ROI.

"We've been measuring the value of the network, and figuring out how to differentiate it and put metrics against it."

Cork Innovates Partnership uses metrics besides jobs and startups. Finn looks at both tangible and intangible measures. Consider these:

- $ Sponsorship income raised on an annual basis
- # Media mentions
  - Means solid event and right speakers
  - Need resource pool for limited budget
- # Events
- # Entrepreneurs reached through the network and connections within the network
  - Demonstrates group rather than working in isolation
- Telling the story
  - Take pride as a team at the local level
- Strength through relationships

Through the process, Cork Innovates Partnership has learned a few other lessons about measuring impact when you are coordinating a network, rather than providing direct services.

"The issue on measurement is that you can't tie everything you do back to job creation goals. We support the organizations that can measure job creation. Their job is to create jobs on a daily basis.

"You must just get started. As you grow reputation and build sphere of influence it extends the ability to deliver impacts, gain credibility and funding."

Research as a Catalyst

In many communities, the first step in identifying resources is research or a report. And that's great … so long as that report doesn't get released with a lot of hype and then relegated to a shelf. In North Carolina and Grand Valley, Michigan, research provided a focal point around which communities rallied to take action.

North Carolina

Deb Markley is the managing director of the Center for Rural Entrepreneurship and has been working in rural communities for most of her career.

"Let me focus on North Carolina because I think there are some interesting things that happened from the state down to communities. At the state level, North Carolina was fortunate to have the North Carolina Rural Center.

"In the mid-2000s, the leader of the Rural Center saw the increased attention being given to entrepreneurship and asked two questions: Who's responsible for doing something about entrepreneurship in the state? Is this something we should be interested in from the standpoint of rural communities?

"Billy Ray Hall (then Rural Center director) commissioned some research, 26 focus groups with entrepreneurs all across the state, all parts of the state. At the end of the day what we found is that entrepreneurs said, 'You don't know what you're doing. We have no idea where to go for help. It's like an alphabet soup out there. You ought to get your act together. It's not just about the money.'

"So the Rural Center brought together the service providers who were supposed to be helping entrepreneurs and shared this research. We had people at the state level, 40 or 50. And we talked about what the entrepreneurs said.

"That group of folks realized that they didn't work together very well and that didn't make sense. That group started meeting monthly, then moved to quarterly and now have been meeting for 10 years. Nobody owns this alliance or network. Somebody hosts a brown bag lunch ... totally informal. They come together, they talk about what's new, lots of partnerships have happened.

"Had the Rural Center not had us do the research and had the Rural Center not had some political cachet, it would not have gotten off on the strong footing it did. They needed to hear from the customer that they were not working together. They needed an intermediary to throw down the gauntlet, call the meeting.

"To me, that's what's been most powerful. Someone – it could have been a foundation, a chamber, a new economic development person – saying, 'Let's bring everyone together and talk about what we're doing, and why we're doing it and how we're doing it and can we do it better.' I think the lessons really resonate in the communities."

Grand Valley

Grand Valley, Michigan, also used research to inspire community action, according to Kevin McCurren, who is on the faculty at the Center for Entrepreneurship and Innovation at Grand Valley State University.

"We were coming out of the economic crisis and west Michigan was saying, 'we need to do something, we've lost the entrepreneurial spirit.' Grand Valley (State University) completed a study called Empowering Entrepreneurship.

"We did a look at what we thought were critical leading factors, whether we were creating new business, looked at culture, a lot of data points about new company formation, patents. When we compared ourselves to other cities of like size we found ourselves non-existent.

"A community survey led to the same thing. Entrepreneurship was not a chosen path. So the university used that study and released it to the community. (The research) coalesced a lot of partners around it. Based upon that we started working with the local government, local corporate partners, economic development organizations looking at places that had been successful at reinstilling a spirit of entrepreneurship.

"The communities that were doing it well realized there were three layers of economic development: chambers, which helped and advocated for existing business; the economic develop arm built around corporate attraction; and a third layer around startups. That's the model we took in Western Michigan.

"When we started looking around we found some commonalities, and so we structured a plan to implement a number of things. One was a centralized place where entrepreneurs could easily find out what was happening.

"Before you change anything, you have to change the culture. We had to make sure our newspapers, our boards, our leaders were supportive of building an entrepreneurial community.

"I think it has to be entrepreneur focused. It has to be flexible in terms of access to assistance. It has to be entrepreneurial in nature, and has to be non-judgmental. Everybody who wants to should have a chance to enter the system and have a fair shot to play. Those who can survive the process, those are the ones we support.

"I find a lot of places in early stages trying to be selective as to who gets in. It should be open to anybody and everybody. There's a place for inventors. It's part of the ecosystem. There needs to be a place for neighborhood-based entrepreneurs.

"We just happened to be at the right time at the right place. A crisis is a terrible thing to waste."

Leadership tip:

Just because you can measure or count something doesn't mean it's important. Figure out what matters in your community. You may have to create your own data collection systems or develop deep partnerships to get the information you need. It's worth it. Real data can drive decision making, tell a compelling story and encourage support.

How do you find the support to identify, connect, empower and measure? Funders look for projects that fit their mission, ignite their passion and follow a straightforward formula.

Section 3

7. FUNDING YOUR SUPPORT NETWORK

"I would like to see additional funding for entrepreneurial development programs."

-U.S. Rep. Steve Chabot of Ohio

"If you can provide the funding and you get the leadership, you'll have a competitive team."

-T. Boone Pickens, Jr., business magnate and financier

The most frequent question we get is how does a community find funding to support building and encouraging an entrepreneurial infrastructure? And it does require funding. The connections and collaborations don't happen by chance. Someone needs to wake up every morning and care about the network.

Step by Step: Maria's Rules for Fundraising

Funding is very straight forward.

1. You have to have a problem.
2. You have to have the data that proves you have the problem.
3. You need to come up with a viable solution that people believe will solve the problem.
4. You need to involve partners.
5. You need to have match dollars to prove the partners are really in it.
6. And you need to be able to tell a clear story that will drive results.

Once you get the funding, it's critical that you execute and show defined results. Success begets success. Getting funding and being successful attracts more funding. It's all in the execution. The key is getting the first grant and knocking it out of the ballpark.

Ask for Enough Funding

Few companies are 100 percent fully sustainable in three years. If you are thinking about launching a new project, you should consider getting at least three years' runway so you can make it sustainable. Make sure you have a well-defined gap you are going to fill. The only way a project will be sustainable is if you are filling a gap. It's the same as a new company going into a market. If a new company doesn't meet the needs of the market, it isn't going to be sustainable. It's the same with a new program.

Why are partnerships important? Because when you get turned down by a potential funder, you want them to understand they're not just turning down your organization, but they are turning down your entire community. It will make it very hard for them to turn you down.

Think about your funding request as a business plan. We're seeing more funders looking for this type of submissions for grants. Funders want to know who's going to manage the project, what do the financials look like, what's the product, how does it fit the market, what are you trying to accomplish and what the results will be. Many funders have taken a return on investment approach to their grant making.

Finding the Right Funder

People buy from people they have a relationship with, so engage with potential funders before you ask for assistance. You need to understand from the funder what's in it for the funder. What is the funder trying to accomplish? How can you help funders hit their goals and make the funders look good? Some funders fund certain things and not others. Don't waste your time going to the wrong funders. Understand their passion, what is it they're trying to accomplish to fulfill their mission, how what you do fits with that. This suggests that you are talking to funders, getting to know them and their mission, long before you make an ask.

Many traditional funding sources are reluctant to fund underlying operations. They tend to be more interested in programs and projects. SourceLink affiliates, all of which are building infrastructure, have been creative in finding funding sources. Frequently the funds come from city, state or county agencies. Examples include: City of Baltimore, Winston-Salem Chamber of Commerce, Loudoun County Economic Development,

Iowa Economic Development Authority and Mississippi Development Authority. JPMorgan Chase, through its foundation, has provided support in select metros where it has a strong presence. In the past, chambers of commerce have stepped up with support.

With the changing nature of federal, state and local funding, many economic development organizations are looking to philanthropy to support their efforts.

The International Economic Development Council (IEDC) published an excellent report in 2016 on philanthropic organizations as potential partners and funding sources for economic development.[21]

"Motivated by the desire to achieve sustainable outcomes, philanthropies and charitable organizations are now seeking to affect change by focusing on comprehensive programs that address the root causes of social problems ... this often intersects with the missions of economic development organizations (EDOs) and can complement the economic growth strategies employed by EDOs."

-Building the Foundation: EDOs and Philanthropies as Partners – IEDC

Other key findings of the report, which surveyed IEDC's full database of members and non-members:

- More than a third of survey respondents received financial or in-kind support from a foundation
- 54 percent of those receiving funding from philanthropic sources were public-private partnerships; 21 percent were private (chambers, public utility companies, etc.) and 25 percent were public state, county or city EDOs
- 51 percent of the survey respondents received funding from community foundations

Another report, *Foundations Leading through Entrepreneurship,*[22] cites the reasons foundations invest in entrepreneurship:

- To bolster and sustain the local philanthropic sector by supporting future philanthropists

[21] Mishka Parkins and Wilson Kerr. "Building the Foundation: EDOs and Philanthropies as Partners." International Economic Development Council, 2016.

[22] Caroline Pringle and Lili Torok. "Foundations Leading through Entrepreneurship." Endeavor Insight, 2015.

- To promote job creation and economic growth, particularly in areas with high rates of poverty
- To empower underserved communities and groups, including women, minorities and immigrants
- To enrich quality of life and prevent brain drain

Foundations

The Burton D. Morgan Foundation, in cooperation with the Foundation Center, has published a mini-directory of foundations that support entrepreneurship, by state. The list, which features almost 100 foundations, can be found at http://www.entre-ed.org/network/funders.pdf.

Local corporations are often a good source of funding. Most corporations have two areas from which they can pull funding: a community relations budget and a marketing budget. If you are able to build a large audience for what you are doing, you may be able to appeal to the marketing arm of the organization.

SourceLink started as KCSourceLink in Kansas City with initial funding from the Kauffman Foundation. Today the KCSourceLink affiliate is partially funded by 12 of Kansas City's largest corporations that have each committed $12,500 for five years. This funding was used as match to access a grant from the U.S. Economic Development Administration.

Federal grants

Federal grants offer opportunities for specific programs. The U.S. Department of Commerce through the Economic Development Administration has funded several initiatives to encourage entrepreneurship and innovation. In rural communities, the Department of Agriculture also can be a resource.

At the federal level, many of the opportunities focus on jobs, distressed communities and the disadvantaged. Recently there seems to be a preference for partnerships and grant requests that include multiple players and collaborations. Go to www.grants.gov for current funding opportunities.

Individuals

Don't discount asking individuals for support. According to Giving USA, in 2015 individuals accounted for 71 percent of charitable giving in the United States. Peter Frumkin, in the book *Strategic Giving: The Art and Science of Philanthropy*,[23] cites five factors that encourage people to donate: change, innovation, equity, pluralism and self-expression. It's not too hard to tie those values to support for entrepreneurship. Maybe your community has a few successful entrepreneurs who are ready to give back.

Philanthropic Funding to Support Entrepreneurship

Pam Lewis is the director of the New Economy Initiative (NEI) at the Community Foundation for Southeast Michigan. That region, including Detroit, conceived a bold idea to fund and support entrepreneurship as a means to strengthen the region's economy.

"The story goes back to 2006 and 2007. The leader of the Community Foundation and its board members started having a conversation, asking what might the region do to position itself for what's coming next in the economy, and how can we make sure we have a talent base and industries that can participate in a global economy.

"Mariam Noland (current president of the Community Foundation for Southeast Michigan), along with a few key board members, were the ones who conceived this thing. She has a big platform and used that to make the case. (They) convinced Ford, Kellogg, Kresge, Knight and six other smaller foundations to put up $100 million to see what philanthropy might do in economic development. They raised the first fund and worked with the partnering foundations to hire researchers to study what was going on, to write the white papers, and to put in place a staff.

"The objective was to understand the role that entrepreneurship could play to diversify the economy and change the culture of our region. How could we reactivate the entrepreneurial DNA of the community and provide ways to support and sustain entrepreneurs?

"In a nutshell, we've been working to sustain this support network…using NEI's grant making capacity to move strategic grants in a very effective way. We fly above individual organizations that support our region's entrepreneurs with business planning, capital and other resources, and we help them see themselves as part of the larger process. Collecting

[23] Peter Frumkin. "Strategic Giving: The Art and Science of Philanthropy." University of Chicago Press, 2006.

data from all our grantees gives us a better sense of what's actually happening in the entrepreneurial community.

"Another key part of NEI's work is its focus on inclusion. We felt as a philanthropy we wanted to talk about inclusion, from empowering more women and minorities to become entrepreneurs to lifting up the role of small and lifestyle businesses in creating healthy communities. It's a grassroots-to-high-growth approach to create opportunity for all. As we made grants, we amplified the conversation about inclusion.

"Another thing we experimented with was the role that challenges and competitions could play in drawing more people to resources like capital and business support. It's not just to draw more people in but also to begin collecting pictures and stories that promote and showcase what is happening to incent more participation. You show people images and share stories, and they can see that entrepreneurship isn't just about young hipsters starting tech companies. It's also about people of different ages, different colors and different genders transforming communities.

"We've made a little over $100 million in grants to support hundreds of programs. We did very few multi-year grants; most are made each year. We have a very robust evaluation process. At the end of 2015 we actually asked for not just aggregate data, but can you give us the client list so we can see for ourselves the synergies? As a result, we were able to better understand the impact of our investments – how that led to jobs and economic impact. The bottom line is, with entrepreneurship, it takes a village … all the touches help the company."

In 2016 the New Economy Initiative commissioned PricewaterhouseCoopers LLP and the W.E. Upjohn Institute for Employment Research to measure the economic and employment impact of its $96.2 million in grants since 2007. That investment resulted in direct assistance to more than 4,400 companies, the launch of more than 1,600 companies, the creation of 17,490 jobs and the generation of nearly $3 billion in real economic output.[24]

The Second Chapter: Tapping into Successful Entrepreneurs

Funding and support for components of the entrepreneurial infrastructure can come from successful entrepreneurs in your community.

---

[24] New Economy Initiative. "IMPACT: Report of the New Economy Initiative," 2016. Retrieved July 2017. http://neweconomyinitiative.org/impact/.

Gerald Smith, meets the definition of successful entrepreneur. For his "second career" he's jumped with both feet into developing a network of coworking spaces (Plexpod.com) in Kansas City, and is in the process of expanding to other cities.

"I was an entrepreneur before people used that word. Back then we just called it being a businessman or business-person. Fortunately, I married Dianna, who is just as entrepreneurial as I am, and she has been an awesome business partner in all our entrepreneurial endeavors for many years now.

"My generation is a rare generation because we got to ride the digital wave. And we built our company around it. I was originally doing sound tracks for film and video, all digital editing stuff. We just jumped in head-first. From there came the web stuff, and we launched a web department. Then all the video production stuff with high definition broadcasting. All these things happened in such a short amount of time, and we were privileged to live through the transition from analog to digital."

Smith's companies were acquired by a global publishing company, and he became president of the acquiring organization. That didn't go well, and he and his wife were unable to buy back the enterprise. So they had a decision to make: *"We can sit back and enjoy life or we keep being who we are. It didn't take more than 45 days to realize that we don't stop, we just keep going. We are entrepreneurs with much to pay forward."*

When working with the publishing company, Smith found himself in the position of trying to do something with excess real estate.

"I came up with the idea of creating an incubator for nonprofits, where you'd bring in a couple of key nonprofits as anchors and we'd respond to this whole millennial movement. Three out of ten millennials want to work for a 'do good' organization or are interested in starting their own. It was a three-year experiment, and it went well.

"Through this process I discovered this trend called coworking, and I thought, 'This is what I've been doing.' We had multiple companies that worked in a sharing economy for 25 years. The web company was different from publishing. We had a teen magazine. All these separate companies shared the same resources. The difference between coworking and what we had done was that all those companies worked for the same employer. In coworking everybody works for different employers. The secret sauce is that collaboration happens when people who work for different employers now work in close proximity to each other.

"I just fell in love with the concept and I thought, 'OK, let's play with this, let's see what happens.' I started getting in touch with people who had a head start. I heard them all say the same thing, you have to be in the urban core, you can't be in the suburbs. So, being the typical entrepreneur that I am, I thought we should prove our model in the suburbs first, let's start with the hardest first.

"We launched the Johnson County (Kansas) facility first. We spent about six weeks working on the branding, Plexpod: plex meaning multiple units, and pod a protective container or housing. It worked, and it reached capacity in four months. It felt a lot like what I'd been doing for 25 years.

"I sometimes say, we're secretly in the business of eliminating distraction and loneliness. You've got to create an environment where services and education come to the entrepreneurs.

"I think what we're doing here is preparing for the generation beyond the millennials, for what the next generation will think about in terms of workforce."

Leadership tip:

Help funders see the results. You have to understand and set realistic expectations. You have to be realistic about solving the problem or closing the gap. Before you even submit a funding request, you should know companies that are going to take advantage of the program and be successful because of your initiative. You should see the benefits before you ever ask for the money.

With Digital Sandbox KC (a proof-of-concept program), we knew three or four companies that would really benefit from proof-of-concept funding and prove the concept. You have to see the results you can achieve ahead of time. You ought to be able to tangibly see something and, if you can, it will help you tell the story. If you can't see it, maybe there's no market or the process/solution is wrong.

One powerful aspect of linking resources is the ability to tell the story of entrepreneurship in your community more effectively. A group working together, telling the same story, will be heard more than a single, lone voice.

8. TELLING THE STORY

Stories spark emotions. We have an intuitive, emotional side as well as a deliberate, rational side to our character. Too often in business we only try and connect with people on a rational level but this isn't enough to actually change how people behave. People may understand what you want them to do but if they aren't emotionally engaged they just won't do it!

-The Storytellers website

Stories are about collaboration and connection. They transcend generations, they engage us through emotions, and they connect us to others. Through stories we share passions, sadness, hardships and joys. We share meaning and purpose. Stories are the common ground that allows people to communicate, overcoming our defenses and our differences. Stories allow us to understand ourselves better and to find our commonality with others.

-*Psychology Today*, The Psychological Power of Storytelling

Look at any active, vibrant entrepreneurial community and you'll see a lot of stories and hear a lot of buzz. Communities like these share the good news to encourage current entrepreneurs, inspire future entrepreneurs and create a climate for innovation. In many communities, the story is fragmented because no one thinks about the message from a community-wide perspective.

One powerful aspect of linking resources is the ability to tell the story of entrepreneurship in your community more effectively. A group working together, telling the same story, will be heard more than a single, lone voice.

Where do you start? With the story.

In each community, the story will be a bit unique. But you can develop the message by asking a few questions:

- What is your goal? What change do you want to make in your community? The purpose of story is to stimulate our imaginations, lead us to action and help us reach our potential.
- Who are the entrepreneurial heroes? Who has started and grown an interesting/thriving company?

- What are the gaps? What does the entrepreneurial community need? What data do you have to prove that need?
- What are the big things happening around entrepreneurship? (1 Million Cups, a new accelerator, a new angel fund)

Once you've developed your story lines, share the messages broadly throughout your network. It's like telling stories around the campfire … shared stories strengthen our connections and change our behaviors.

Then, as you consider how to share this information with the broader community, it's back to the basics of marketing.

Step by Step: Telling the Story

1. Who's the audience?
2. What's the objective?
3. What's the message?
4. How will you reach your audience?

Who's the Audience?

In most communities there are a variety of audiences who will want to hear your stories or, at the very least, you will want them to hear your stories. These audiences typically include:

- Entrepreneurial support organizations
- Entrepreneurs, startups and aspiring business owners
- Other business supporters such as bankers, accountants and lawyers
- Investors
- Community leaders, philanthropists, potential funders
- Local and state legislators and elected leaders

What's the Objective?

You may have a slightly different objective with each audience. Overall, it may be to support the entrepreneurial infrastructure. For support organizations, that may mean joining and participating in a connected network. For entrepreneurs, it may be taking full advantage of the resources available. You may want other business supporters to connect their clients to your network. For investors, community leaders and elected officials, it may be financial support.

It may be helpful to create a matrix (Figure 15) with each audience listed in a vertical column, and objective, message and strategy on the horizontal row. That way you can start to identify the specifics for each audience. In marketing, one size hardly ever fits all.

Audience	Objective	Message	Strategy
Entrepreneurs	Links to resources	Find what you need	Social media
Investors	Educate re: early-stage	Find opportunity	Small gatherings

Figure 15: Marketing matrix

What's the Message?

It makes sense that if you want different audiences to do different things, the message may also be slightly different. Sometimes it's a case of taking a strong core message (the number of entrepreneurs reached by your network in a given year) and spinning the story a bit differently. For the support organizations, the message is about a job well done. For the entrepreneurs, you can focus more on the variety of services available and how smart it is to use the services. Funders will be most interested in whether their dollars are making a difference.

Crafting clear, compelling messages is an art. Focus on the information most likely to lead the audience to doing the thing you've said you want them to do (the objective). Talk to them and about them. Talk in terms of benefits for them, not features of your program.

How Will Your Reach Your Audience?

To deliver any message effectively, you have to know how your audience looks for the answers to the problems you solve: Where do they hang out?

How do they get and process information? What do they respond to? What motivates them to take action?

If you don't know the answers to these questions, ask your audience, just like you would ask customers about preferred marketing channels.

The most effective communication is the most personal. Don't print a brochure when the audience is small enough that you can communicate by phone or email. The most scalable communication is organic: use inbound marketing (i.e., earning your audience's attention organically without interrupting anyone's path) to really engage your audience when they're looking for answers to the problems you solve. This includes anything from search engine optimization to video content to public speaking to community building.

A Few Tips about Using Social Media Effectively

Social media is just one marketing channel you can use to reach your audience where they are and where they're having conversations about the services you may provide.

One of the advantages of social media is that it allows you to listen to and interact with your audiences vs. talking at them. Your audiences are made up of people, and people want to be listened to and engaged with. With social media you're not pitching an agenda, you're joining a conversation.

Using social media, you can:

- Build visibility quickly (and relatively cheaply)
- Spark and track conversations
- Create and cultivate relationships with new and diverse audiences
- Establish trust and expertise (remember "Know, Like, Trust, Buy"?)
- Solve problems

How do you start? Sarah Mote, director of marketing for SourceLink, offers these tips:

Listen:

- Who is your current audience and how do they already interact with you?

- Monitor hot topics and key influencers. Who already has the ear of your customer?
- Find out where your customers, influencers and stakeholders are. Don't spend time on channels where your target audiences aren't or where you can't achieve your business goals.
- Understand the discourse. Find out how people use the channel to interact, what they talk about, what they are interested in. Don't be that person who talks about insurance premiums at a birthday party.

Plan:

- How will social media help you reach your business goals? Is it impressions (brand awareness), reach (customer engagement) or clicks (website traffic and conversions)? What will you measure?
- Use your "listening" and your business goals to create an editorial calendar of key community events, your speaking and outreach engagements and your audiences' expressed concerns and questions.
- Create your content marketing plan: How can you turn conversations into conversions, however you define that for your organization? What messages will resonate with your audience? What action do you want your audience to take? How can you have a deeper conversation with your customer and connect them with the help you provide, via website, blog, ebook, video, etc.?

Engage:

- Be a human: People connect with people, not brands. Build relationships and trust.
- Be present and know the culture of the channel you're using. Adjust your message to the social media channel (Facebook is not LinkedIn) and be responsive.
- Create shareable content that is about your customers – not about you. Be useful and let your fans be useful and smart by giving them content that they want to share forward.
- Image is everything: Pins, tweets, posts with images and videos get more traction than those that don't. But do be sure you own or have the commercial rights to any photos you post.

Entrepreneurs in Action

KCSourceLink has been hearing and sharing the stories of KC

entrepreneurs since 2003. A few years ago, the Entrepreneurs in Action blog was officially launched. The blog was a spinoff of stories that were featured in KCSourceLink's annual report, We Create KC. The blog shares diverse stories of entrepreneurship in Kansas City. A glance at the list will show that all types of entrepreneurs are featured, from makers and shakers to cinnamon roll bakers.

This approach not only provides content for KCSourceLink to leverage, but also provides additional exposure for the entrepreneurs featured and helps fulfill KCSourceLink's mission of telling the story of entrepreneurship.

These stories are leveraged through social media, with links back to the original stories. Since the segment was launched, nearly 200 profiles have been featured. It continues to be a popular part of www.kcsourcelink.com, generating more than 20,000 pageviews in 2016 and ranking as one of the top five entry points into the website.

Telling Your Own Story

If you are looking for ways to tell the story of your organization specifically, here are a few ideas:

Battle of the Brands

First launched in March 2012, the KCSourceLink Battle of the Brands was designed to help shine the spotlight on Kansas City entrepreneurship and promote the businesses that start and grow there. The idea was simple: a bracket-style competition with 64 entrepreneurs and iconic brands, with fans voting for pairs in each round until one company emerged as the champion. The timing, of course, was chosen to coincide with the NCAA tournament.

Mote tells the story of how this project grew from a simple idea into a web-traffic-generating phenomenon.

"We started with simple criteria. We wanted to make sure all types of entrepreneurs could play. We looked for companies with entrepreneurial roots in the Kansas City metro region, in business for at least one year and showing evidence of growth and innovation. The last criterion was purely subjective.

"The first year we nominated companies to play internally. We gathered our staff and Resource Partners and asked for names of companies they worked with. After that, we took public nominations and had a play-in, seeding round. After the first year, we had enough response to divide entries into the brackets of Main Street, Innovation-led, Second Stage and Microenterprise. For the most part, this pitted firms of similar size against each other, and it allowed us to declare four "bracket" winners in addition to the overall champion. There was no entry fee and the only prizes were bragging rights and a pair of boxing gloves that we gave to the winner.

"We were amazed and thrilled at how quickly the companies jumped on board, using social media to promote their journey to the top spot. There were good natured trash talk tweets, inspirational videos and, our favorite, the Dolce Bakery flour-tagging of their competitors' walls (Figure 16). The big tear jerker, though: several companies entered into collaborations based on their engagement with each other in the battle. In a few instances, Battle of the Brands turned competitor into customer.

Figure 16: Dolce Bakery flour-tags the competition in Battle of the Brands

"The idea was to spark conversations around entrepreneurship, drive traffic to the KCSourceLink website and help us connect with and educate at least 64 companies about what we do at KCSourceLink. Battle of the Brands did all that and more. In 2017, the Battle accounted for more than 10 percent of our overall website traffic, 16 percent of incoming local traffic and blew up our social media. The Battle let us engage with our entrepreneurs in a really unique and fun way, and helped them promote their businesses."

Tap into existing events

In many communities there are already events going on … TechWeek, Startup Week, Global Entrepreneurship Week. It's usually not too hard to get involved and use the event's network to leverage your story.

1. Join the conversation on social media, using the event's hashtag, e.g., #NationalSmallBusinessWeek or #GEWUSA. Comment on

what's happening and talk about your own activities.

2. Co-host an event, working with the organizers, to showcase your resources and your network. Back it up with content marketing and social media engagement.
3. Prepare your community for the event and guide them to local resources through your content: blog posts, videos, newsletters, event calendar, ebooks. Encourage your partner resources to contribute and share.

Leadership tip:

Stories must spark emotion. Go deeper than just the headline or the tweet. Talk about the real people who are starting and growing companies in your community. You won't have to look far for a compelling story … they are all around you.

Building an entrepreneurial network is, at its heart, a work of collaboration and community change. And that kind of endeavor requires a very special kind of leader, one who knows how to build bridges, engage a very broad community, nurture relationships and get everyone focused on the really "big hairy audacious goal."

9. IT TAKES A LEADER: HOW TO GET IT STARTED AND KEEP IT GOING

"It comes down to leadership. You have to say it's a priority and we're going to make it happen."

-Dell Gines, senior community development advisory
Federal Reserve Bank of Kansas City

By the time you finish reading this chapter, you may decide you want nothing to do with trying to build an entrepreneurial infrastructure in your community. What we are talking about is community and cultural change. It takes a very special kind of leadership.

No one will follow you because of your position in an organization. No one will get involved because you head a task force. No one will move things forward because you pen a beautiful strategic plan.

And it gets worse.

People will grab the spotlight. (Let them.) They will take credit for your ideas. (Be willing to share.) They will steal your funding (OK, maybe don't let them do that). Some days you'll feel like nothing is changing. Jim Brasunas with ITEN in St. Louis calls it "pushing the rock uphill."

And now we'll tell you the good part: in 20 years or so, you'll look back and see that you were part of something amazing, and that you helped sow and nurture the seeds of change and economic vitality in your community.

Building an entrepreneurial network is, at its heart, a work of collaboration and community change. And that kind of endeavor requires a very special kind of leader, one who knows how to build bridges, engage a very broad community, nurture relationships and get everyone focused on the really "big hairy audacious goal."

We're talking about change management. Change management requires a few key things. You need a problem that needs to be solved. You have to find a solution that people believe is viable. You have to stick behind it throughout implementation. You have to have folks who are able to pull it off, and everybody involved needs to believe they have something to be gained from the process.

As we've worked with amazing leaders around the United States, we've found that many have these kinds of qualities:

- Entrepreneurial – see opportunities, plan and execute, rally resources, adjust to the marketplace
- Collaborative
- Driven
- Inquisitive
- Successful in communications
- Great listeners
- Selfless

The people who support entrepreneurship and small business have to be every bit as entrepreneurial and business-minded as the clients they serve. They have to know how to find opportunities, demonstrate value and rally resources.

Entrepreneurship is a contact sport. It takes time and energy – that's why most people don't engage in it. In most communities building an entrepreneurial support network has been left to the nonprofit section … working in the white space between the government and the private sector.

Some offices have these great motivational posters around the room. If you're building entrepreneurial infrastructure, here are a few posters that you should consider for your office:

- Lead from behind
- Be entrepreneurial
- Collaborate, collaborate, collaborate
- Relationships matter
- Diversity matters
- Execution is everything

Lead from Behind

The term "servant leadership" was coined by Robert K. Greenleaf in his 1970 essay *The Servant as Leader*.

"The servant-leader is servant first … It begins with the natural feeling that one wants to serve, to serve first. Then conscious choice brings one to aspire to lead. That person is sharply different from one who is a leader first, perhaps because of the need to assuage an unusual power drive or to acquire material possessions … A servant-leader focuses primarily on the growth and well-being of people and the communities to which they belong … The servant-leader shares power, puts the needs of others first and helps people develop and perform as highly as possible."

Being a servant leader, leading from behind, means letting others take the credit. It means convincing others that your ideas are their ideas, or creating ideas together. It means caring much more about the community, the partners you work with, the entrepreneurs you serve than any credit you will ever get.

In the book *From Good to Great*, Jim Collins calls this Level 5 leadership. In his research, he found that truly great leaders have humility and share credit for success. He noted that great leaders don't seek success for their own glory, but recognize that success is critical for the team.

You have to give first.

When you're starting from scratch, and you can see groups that are moving things forward, amplifying their work can be one of the best ways to build the whole system. Also when you're working with volunteers – which you're going to be – you are going to find people with passion who have connections and can make things happen. You need to put some support under them to make those things happen. Some of what you have to do is seed the system, and sometimes that means doing things you don't get paid for.

Deb Markley of the Center for Rural Entrepreneurship has seen the importance of effective leadership in her years of work in rural communities.

"(An effort) doesn't go very far if you don't have a few local champions. It's just too easy to write off someone who's not from that place, doesn't have real community ownership. Someone has to own it and take it to the next step. It just doesn't go very far without those champions."

She said different people champion entrepreneurship in a community for different reasons. As one example, she cites the head of a community foundation:

"He has a bigger vision for the community. He sees that they aren't likely to have another

big business come in. He can say, 'Entrepreneurship is what we need to focus on to drive the economy.'

"Other places, it comes from entrepreneurs. They are really committed to building their own business in this place, and they care enough about the community that they want other people to do the same thing. They recognize that they are not competitive with other businesses, but see that if we had more, we'd be better off. People want to build a sector.

"And finally there's that person who just really cares about the community. They've just lived in the community for a long time and want it to be better. One of the early champions we saw in a North Carolina community was a guy who called every high school football game and every high school basketball game. Not an entrepreneur, but he had deep, deep roots and saw that the community could be supportive of people building businesses. As a volunteer, he provided strong leadership for a community team that was taking the first steps toward organizing a support system for local businesses. Ultimately, that effort led to the creation of a network for entrepreneurs and local business owners."

ImagineU

Mike Hoffmeyer, director of the University of Memphis Crews Center for Entrepreneurship, saw collaboration as the critical element in a new program, ImagineU. ImagineU is a collaboration of seven teaching institutions that include a historically black college, community college, college of art, college of music, private college and public university.

The 12-week pilot course launched during the summer of 2015 with a focus on accepting a diverse and equal number of students from the seven institutions. The program provides a rich experience for entrepreneurial-minded students.

Some of the students may not immediately choose an entrepreneurial career path, but the program is designed to instill an entrepreneurial mindset. Hoffmeyer describes the program as a "supercharged" internship designed to "prime the pump." Based on initial success, the institutions modified the program and have been able to raise additional corporate funding support.

Be Entrepreneurial

Since there's no established infrastructure (yet) for entrepreneurship, anybody that gets into this business has to come up with new solutions, which means they have to be entrepreneurial. They have to find creative ways to fund the solutions they come up with.

St. Louis has been gaining recognition as a "hot spot" for entrepreneurship. Much of that "overnight" success dates back to 2008 and the beginnings of ITEN. Jim Brasunas, ITEN founder, describes how he tried to follow the advice he gives entrepreneurs in terms of approaching a market. He listened to his customers, found a gap to fill, tried some things (that did and didn't work) and started small.

"We started ITEN in 2008, and St. Louis had really nothing going for tech startups at that time. I was previously involved trying to put together a tech incubator (Technology Entrepreneur Center). Wow, talk about pushing the rock up a hill. Nobody was interested.

"Then, at the same time we were winding down TEC, another organization, Innovate St. Louis, was coming out of the woodwork. One of the clusters they were going after was information technology. Innovate got some seed money from the State of Missouri to start a new program for tech startups and drafted me to head it up … ITEN was born.

"At the beginning it was just me … My advantage from my days at TEC was I knew a bunch of entrepreneurs in the region. I started going around talking to the entrepreneurs, asking what they needed, what they were doing.

"They all said, 'I need money and there are no investors here in St. Louis who are willing to get involved because they don't understand it. And I'm the only tech entrepreneur for a thousand miles around, and what plane do I get on to California, because that's my only chance of doing anything.'

"They all thought they were the only ones. I started talking to some investors, and they said, 'The only deals are in California. I go out there once a year.' So it dawned on me that these people are probably sitting on the same planes going out to California. There's something wrong with this picture.

"I invited two dozen tech entrepreneurs to a happy hour. I had everybody stand in a big circle and went around the room. Each one said what they were trying to do with their company. They all simultaneously had this epiphany that they had a peer group. That was really the beginning.

"I started trying to find out how best to link these people to mentors who had something to offer. Any time you are trying to start a program where you are going to have people giving advice, the mentors that you pick are really, really critical. If you pick typical retired business executives to work with tech entrepreneurs, they're not going to speak the same language.

"Little by little, I designed programs. First thing we did was a mentor match. Then we did a speed dating with investors. That was good in that I learned that kind of format was not going to work. There was a lot of trial and error to see what worked.

"We stumbled onto one program … one of our startup companies came to us and said, 'I've got these investors that I'm meeting with next week. Can you pull a few mentors together to look at my presentation?' It was such a valuable experience for the entrepreneur, and the mentors really enjoyed it too. That's where the Mock Angel program came from.

"The Mock Angel program has been a cornerstone of ITEN since then. We average about 8-12 graduates from that program a year. It's very rigorous. We also added a parallel track of due diligence, not only getting the story and pitch deck together, but also running the traps with documentation. They have to get a green light from both sides to graduate."

And from there, Brasunas added a prequel program (Business Model Validation), more mentoring, entrepreneurs-in-residence and a corporate engagement initiative. The secret: *"You've got to approach it entrepreneurially."*

Collaborate, Collaborate, Collaborate

In real estate, it's location, location, location. In community change, it's all about collaboration.

A fundamental part of what we do at SourceLink is empower the communities we work with to take a risk and collaborate with their peers, resulting in significant returns for the entrepreneurial community. As we've said before, it's not always easy to collaborate. Everyone wants to lead. People have different agendas. Sometimes fear plays a role.

Set all that aside and jump in. Invite a few people to work with you on a project. Be very clear about the vision, the expected outcome, the destination. Find that tiny spark of collaboration and tend it carefully. You'll be amazed at how often it only takes one spark to set off a wildfire.

Markley also has a few words about collaboration:

"Collaboration is not the most natural thing to do. The work we're asking people to do, this collaborative coming together work, you have to appeal to people's individual interest.

"One of the principles is that people come to the table and stay at the table based on their individual interest. Eventually they may see a common interest. That's not about greed or selfishness, it's a fact of life. If this is going to make me better at the job I have

to do, I'm much more likely to commit time and effort to it.

"Who are the stakeholders? Why do they care? Why would someone sit down with someone else? It's that kind of thinking that communities need to do more of ... we're finding that in entrepreneurial communities in North Carolina, those communities heading into the second year of building ecosystems are starting to recognize that ... not everyone has to come to every meeting. What do you care about? Then that's what we'll ask you to do. Speak to what jazzes you up because that will keep you at the table."

Dr. Joseph Picken has been teaching entrepreneurship and supporting the entrepreneurial infrastructure in Dallas since the late 1990s, after a more than 30-year career in industry and consulting. He is the founder of the academic program and the founder and academic director of the Institute for Innovation and Entrepreneurship at The University of Texas at Dallas. When he started looking at the landscape in Dallas, he saw a lot of silos.

"Nobody was working with anyone else ... Everyone in the community was competing, everyone wanted to do everything ... I spent three or four years just preaching collaboration. We eventually got to a point where we each focused on what we did well and worked with each other. Out of that came a number of programs.

"When the Institute was founded 12 years ago, everyone was trying to do everything for entrepreneurs in the community. After a lot of pounding on the table, we got people to agree that, 'We can't do it all, we have to work together, we have to stop competing, we have to share resources and refer people to our associates.' We now tend to work together reasonably well.

"That has worked well for more than ten years. We now have a more collaborative environment and have launched a number of accelerators and coworking spaces. It's not perfect by any means. There's still not a lot of coherence. It's still a bit fragmented.

"At the state level, in 2008, we launched TUNIE (Texas University Network for Innovation and Entrepreneurship). We put together a consortium of academic institutions and medical schools as members of a Texas network."

TUNIE had four broad goals: Provide education, outreach and support across Texas; support the commercialization of university technologies; encourage collaboration among its members; and increase government awareness and recognition of the contribution of its programs to innovation and economic development.

"We've done a pretty good job on three out of four. We haven't done a very good job of increasing awareness within the government. We've fallen back to an annual meeting and

sharing best practices. The real value has been the relationships. We work collectively on projects, but mostly we share ideas and best practices.

"Bottom line, I think collaboration is really critical. This is important work and there's a lot to be done. If we work together rather than competing with each other, we can continue to make good progress."

Relationships Matter

Frank and Kimberlee Spillers founded Global Horizons to revitalize rural America. Their work has strengthened rural communities for 30 years. In their experience, what brings results is relationships.

"Projects have their place, but growth will happen more quickly when you build civility by building relationships. Everything works better when good relationships are present; we call it 'Relationship Economic Development.' Getting to know people from other communities in a region changes the perception of 'we hate that community,' to 'that community has a lot going for it.' Mutual support helps a region thrive and makes processes work better when people have relationships that focus on building civility in all their community organizations and governments.

"It's too easy to 'hate' a general group of people you don't know or a principle or a perception of that group. You can hate an intangible thing. But, when you get to know something or someone on a personal level, it's hard to continue that hate. And when you have a relationship, it's almost impossible to hate that person."

But how do you get people to want to build relationships? How do you get them to the table?

"Those involved have to see a need or an urgency. It can be a school superintendent seeing a decline in students, or a company that finds it hard to get employees. They have to see that the way that they have been doing economic development in the past no longer works. People have to talk about changing the future to do things differently."

In their work, the Spillers use a process called "deliberative dialogue," which focuses on value-based decisions. *"Dialogue allows people to talk about community values and the values of each person to discover 'why' a person thinks the way they do. It's this 'why,' not the 'how' or 'what' you are going to do. Once people talk about values, it changes the discussion. When we go about doing what we are doing based on values and relationship, we improve the environment."*

Frequently, an outside facilitator helps spark and encourage the conversation. But real change in a community happens from the inside.

"It's vital to have an inside sparkplug. The inside person is really the fuel that helps spark the community."

Frank Spillers described one such community catalyst.

"I know an entrepreneur who graduated from high school and started a small shop in a town of 120 people. He built the shop into a multi-million-dollar business. Seeing value in building the region through relationships, he is working to grow population with some ideas he learned from some of our community work. He continues to lead change in that community.

"Relationships matter. That's why we call our approach Relationship Economic Development."

Diversity Begets Diversity

Dell Gines has been speaking about diversity in entrepreneurship for most of his career. He sees diversity as a deliberate action that a community must pursue to make economic opportunity available to everyone in the community.

"Diversity is connected to the concept of social capital. If you look back historically, discrimination and segregation were huge, not just in terms of the physical barriers. We often don't talk about the social capital networks that are so important to business owners and how minorities have been excluded from those networks. And it's not always intentional. People are in relationships that are non-diverse and the networks just replicate that.

"'If we want to develop the capacity of all citizens, we have to have two-way intentionality. Non-diverse networks need to make sure they are reaching out actively to women, ethnic and minority groups. And those who are part of the communities that have not been engaged need to seek out these networks and go through the uncomfortable part of being somewhere new until it becomes normalized.

"The rise of startups in modern America has focused on high-growth entrepreneurs, creating a culture around the startup community of networking and fun, access to financial and human capital. (In these networks) you are around people who have figured out something that you haven't figured out yet, or if you have a question, someone knows someone who can answer it. That's why it's so important for diversity in these networks.

"There's even a linguistic division in this space that kind of segments the high-

growth startup community (which they call entrepreneurship) and small business. Entrepreneurship gets all the attention. African, Hispanic and Native Americans, with a few exceptions, tend to start more traditional businesses.

"So we just need to be intentional about it on both sides. Networks matter. Relationships matter. Diversity matters. We need to focus on how we can make that happen so that we can have a greater distribution of economic growth among all segments.

Diversity begets diversity. The more diverse people you include, the more diverse people will become included in things because they work their own networks for you.

How do you do it?

"On the startup community side, it's literally saying 'we want to be more diverse' and aligning the leadership and major relationships to buy into that. You begin to look for stakeholders and groups that share that same vision and begin to work with them. We can't assume people know how to do diversity. They may feel uncomfortable going into different environments. They may not know where to start.

"Find stakeholders who can introduce you into the community. And communities that are ethnic, minority and women, find out what's happening in the startup space. Say 'This is something we need to participate in to grow new and different kinds of businesses.' That's what I mean about two-way intentionality. Those in the network and those out both need to decide to participate and to co-create a diverse environment."

Execution Is Everything

Defining problems and identifying gaps and writing reports and holding meetings will not move the needle one inch. Leadership guru Warren Bennis said, "Great groups ship." By that he meant that great groups develop a tangible product. They get something done.

One of the hallmarks of the team we've assembled at SourceLink is that we don't let up. We don't just put the report out there and define the problem. We implement the solutions.

You have to have an executor. You can't let up until you get to the end. Which suggests you should know what the end is. You have come up with some measurements so that you know you are moving things forward.

Penny Lewandowski has learned some key lessons in execution in her work with the Greater Baltimore Technology Council and at the Edward Lowe Foundation.

"Execution is critical, particularly when you are working with growth companies. By the time you've finished your fourth focus group, they've moved on to speedier pastures. They're looking for trusted sources and often it's not you. To gain their trust, give them a seat at the table and a voice. Creating a program with no input is a sure path to failure. Understand their needs, then offer what they're not getting someplace else. And when you say you are going to go … go!

"The minute someone starts to duplicate your successful efforts – which they will – be ready for something new. Duplication and silos confuse and frustrate busy entrepreneurs. Be original, get buy-in and then move."

"Anything worth doing is worth getting done."

-Kate Pope Hodel

Messy Is OK

Christi Bell, associate vice provost and executive director of the Business Enterprise Institute at the University of Alaska-Anchorage, tells the story of how a group of committed people with passion came together to make a difference for Anchorage's entrepreneurs.

"The most exciting thing we've done lately is Launch: Alaska, a business accelerator without walls.

"Historically what we've been told was that there was not enough capital in Alaska, and if only we had a bricks and mortar incubator all would be well. A community of folks have been really coming together over the last decade to test that assumption and dig deeper, to find out who needed money and why they weren't getting it.

"We were successful in launching the 49th State Angel Fund in Anchorage. All of a sudden we had capital, but we couldn't get the capital deployed. That caused us to question our assumptions.

"There was a group from the university, from local venture and angel capital groups who joined local entrepreneurs who had an interest in getting higher quality deals, and people thinking about entrepreneurship from a scalable business model perspective.

The first thing they did was to look internally; to ask the question, 'What assets does Alaska have that can be leveraged into highly scalable companies?' Quickly the group settled on energy as a strategic focus area and went to work trying to attract, retain and grow energy innovators.

"Energy is one of the challenges of Alaska, and one of the areas where we felt from a university perspective we had the greatest commercialization potential. We really tried to focus the accelerator on the energy sector, but in the first year we just did a broad recruitment of companies to ensure we filled the cohort.

"We had 44 applications, from across the globe ... (We accepted) 14 into the pre-accelerator and five companies into the full cohort. These teams went through a very intensive experience over the summer. One made pitches at demo day, two received funding within three months and a third received funding within six months. This result exceeded our expectations and is extraordinary for first-year accelerators.

"This really was a community initiative. The Rasmuson Foundation, Native Corporations, GCI, local angel funds and private investors came forward. The Boardroom, which is recognized as one of the top 50 coworking spaces in the country by Paste Magazine, hosted the accelerator. More than 50 community leaders engaged as mentors, and many of the same folks organizing events like Startup Weekend, 1 Million Cups, and business plan competitions all contributed time. The University supported as a sponsor, lending staff to increase operational bandwidth and funding to support programing."

Bell is quick to credit others as the movers behind the project, including founding board members Joe Morrison, Ky Holland, Katherine Jernstrom, Gianna Foltz, Gretchen Fauske, Nolan Klouda and Adam Krynicki. Lance Ahern served as the initial managing director and recently joined the board. Entrepreneurs Andre Horton and Mary Miner recently brought leadership to the board. Isaac Vanderburg, previously executive director of the Alaska Small Business Development Center, is now leading L:A as its new managing director.

The accelerator's fast-paced march to success has drawn attention.

"One of the results is that the Office of Naval Research has committed $200,000 a year for the next three years to push this idea of an energy accelerator. This accelerator was an experiment, but it's gaining traction for sustainability. We are modeling after the Hawaii energy accelerator. They are light years ahead of us but a wonderful model.

"While it created some tensions at times, nobody owned it. Folks came together from

across the community. It's a wonderful example of what can be done when you get a group of committed and passionate people together who have a shared vision. There were a lot of long hours and people feeling burned out. It seemed like when I heard someone had to step back, another member would step forward and fill that gap or engage in a way that we didn't even realize needed to be engaged. It wasn't perfect. Messy is OK.

"What we have in our economy day-to-day right now is pretty negative. This was a committed group of people trying to focus on something positive.

"You don't need bricks and mortar. The care and feeding of that is not always sustainable. I don't have any negativity toward incubators, but for our community, I'm glad we did this accelerator with no walls model.

"Without walls, you can get way more people involved."

We Created a Movement

A bold statement came forth from Kansas City in 2011. The home of jazz and barbecue declared it would be more; it would be America's most entrepreneurial city. Entrepreneurship became one of the Greater Kansas City Chamber of Commerce's "Big 5" Initiatives. Peter deSilva, then president and COO of UMB Financial Corp., stepped up to lead the effort.

But why would the head of one of the largest banks in the region care about entrepreneurship?

"We should all care (about entrepreneurs.) We know that small firms are creating all the net new jobs the United States. Every large firm was once a small firm. The intersection between large and small firms is clearer today than it ever has been.

"Large firms rely on small firms to deliver products that they can't. Large firms are not known for being particularly innovative. Large firms are outsourcing their innovation office to smaller firms that don't have the same boundaries and limitations you find in a larger firm. Smaller firms are willing to take risks that larger firms aren't willing to take.

"If larger firms can help fund and be the first customer, you have an ecosystem that's been created, from innovation and invention to selling the first product to a ready customer.

"For me it was an economic development imperative that we get behind smaller firms and entrepreneurs and rebuild that sense of risk taking in the community.

"When you look at KC, it's historically been home to great entrepreneurs, you can list them all. But at that moment, that juncture in time, the KC economy had stalled out. The vibrancy that was once there had dissipated. There was a recognition by groups like the Chamber, the Kansas City Area Economic Development Council, the Civic Council, that if KC was going to re-emerge as a great center of commerce in the United States, it needed to rebuild its entrepreneurial spirit.

"So for me, this was about economic development, an approach that would be a long term, transformational opportunity for the KC community. One thing was clear: the business community was going to have to step up and lead this. For all the other efforts going on with various organizations, the business community had to mandate that this was going to happen."

While many communities make a commitment to supporting entrepreneurs, few declare that they will become America's most entrepreneurial city.

"I remember that day like it was yesterday, sitting with Carl Schramm (former Kauffman Foundation president) in his office at the Kauffman Foundation. Carl's advice was just claim it, just make it so. Tell the world and then go fill in the gaps. He said, 'No one will challenge you, no one will take you literally.' It was a very bold statement of intent. It took me a little while to get comfortable with it. If somebody called me on it, I couldn't prove it. But it was exciting. That's when I realized we were not driving an initiative, we were creating a movement.

"I thought that was a pivotal moment.

"And declare it we did. We told the country and the world that Kansas City was going to be a great entrepreneurial city in America.

"I shepherded what was beginning to happen. There were sprouts of grass: Startup Village, KCSourceLink. UMKC and the Chamber got interested. There was no central coordination, no one who was bringing it together. Right or wrong, we said we're going to make this (entrepreneurship) one of our Big 5 imperatives for KC. In my mind, that was the tipping point. When big business said, 'We value this, we're going to get involved, we're going to put our shoulders to the grindstone,' that was a game changer.

"When people are sick, you have two choices. You take a painkiller and it feels good for a while or you deal with the root cause of the problem. In KC, we had a lot of treating the symptoms: we'll get some funding, we'll connect people. But the truth was it wasn't any one thing, it was the sum of all those things that we needed to pull the entrepreneurial community into place.

"You can't create an entrepreneurial community, they create themselves. You can create the conditions in which entrepreneurs choose to innovate. You can work across government and universities and private-public partnership lines to make it easier for entrepreneurs to start and grow companies. No single action in and of itself was going to be a panacea. It was a set of coordinated actions that made Kansas City a desirable place for entrepreneurs.

"Kansas City has made remarkable progress over the last few years on things like funding and connecting resources. We've done tremendous work. The community has embraced it. It's kind of hip to be there. Kansas City is winning lots of awards for being the best place for young people.

"The entrepreneurial movement we started is only getting stronger. I can see it every day. I think in the next decade or two KC will be known as America's most entrepreneurial city. That's the goal."

Leadership tip:

Encourage ideas from many sources. This means trying things and not getting too attached to them. If they work, great. If they don't, let go. And at some point a really great thing will run its course and you'll have to bid it a fond farewell. Don't mourn. By letting go, you free up time and energy to move on to something else.

The entrepreneurs will tell you when an idea is bad. They will either not show up or tell you how awful the concept is. And if you are open, they'll give you a lot of ideas for how to make it better. And when it's time to stop doing something, you'll sense that the energy is gone. Celebrate what it was, learn from the experience, and use it as a base to springboard to something with more impact.

Here it is: the glossary we all wanted when we first started working in entrepreneurship. How does an accelerator compare to an incubator?

10. SPEAKING STARTUP: THE JARGON

"If you talk to a man in a language he understands, that goes to his head. If you talk to him in his own language, that goes to his heart."
-Nelson Mandela, former president of South Africa

If you are going to venture somewhere new, it's always good to get familiar with the language. Entrepreneurship support is no different than any other field – it has its own terms and traditions. And the alphabet soup of federal, state and local agencies that play can make you crazy.

We talked with some of the newer associates at SourceLink and asked them what would have been helpful in their early days. They all said a glossary ... so here it is. The definitions are taken from a variety of sources.

Accelerator: An accelerator is a location-based business development program that typically works with cohorts and has a specified program and/or time horizon for education and mentoring. Some accelerators take a small amount of equity, although that is changing.

Angel Investors: High-net-worth individuals who provide capital to high-growth potential startup and early-stage businesses, usually in exchange for equity or convertible debt. Angels generally invest their own money, often making investments in the range of $5,000 to $100,000. Super Angels are experienced investors with greater means than more typical angels. Super Angels invest their own capital or invest larger amounts cooperatively with other like-minded individuals. They often fill the $250,000-$1 million funding gap.

Asset Map: Identifies service offerings in a community organized by the specific services offered and audience served. An asset map can be used to help identify gaps in services offered, allowing service providers, policy makers and funders to effectively allocate resources.

Bankable Companies: Have the collateral, track record and/or cash flow to qualify for conventional bank small business financing. "Nonbankable" companies typically need access to alternative loans or bank guarantees.

Community Development Financial Institutions (CDFI): Private-sector financial intermediaries with community development as their primary mission. While many CDFIs serve as community development banks, they can offer microenterprise funds that provide small amounts of business capital to small scale entrepreneurs.

Community Reinvestment Act (CRA) of 1977: Intended to encourage depository institutions to help meet the credit needs of the communities in which they operate, including low- and moderate-income neighborhoods. Lending institutions can receive favorable CRA consideration for investments in a pool that would be used to make microloans to promote economic development in a regional area that includes the institution's assessment area.

Coworking Spaces: Coworking is a style of work that involves a shared working environment. Many coworking spaces offer a variety of options, such as open space and individual offices, access to meeting rooms and shared services. Frequently usage is based on a membership fee or month-to-month rent.

Debt (Loans): The amount of money borrowed by one party from another. Companies in the startup and growth stages frequently acquire debt (borrow money) to fuel their startup or growth costs. Debt must be repaid and does not provide any company ownership for the lender.

Economic Development Administration (EDA): Part of the U.S. Department of Commerce, promotes innovation and competitiveness through programs and grants.

Economic Development Council, Commission or Corporation (EDC): Usually local organizations dedicated to encouraging economic development in their areas.

Entrepreneurial Ecosystem: An entrepreneurial ecosystem comprises the many and varied components in a community that connect together to create a supportive environment in which people can start and grow successful companies. Those components typically include events; training classes; funding mechanisms; mentoring and coaching; technology transfer groups; incubators; and labs. An entrepreneurial ecosystem also includes connectivity among entrepreneurs; resource providers and investors; a culture that supports risk and innovation; a pipeline of talent; and programs that celebrate entrepreneurs in the community.

Entrepreneur Support Organization (ESO): An organization that provides training, education, counseling or other assistance to entrepreneurs. These organizations are typically nonprofit, government or educational in nature.

Equity: Stock or any other security representing ownership interest. When a company acquires equity funding, it is trading some ownership of the company for the capital.

Grant: Money given to a company that does not have to be repaid and does not require equity in the company to be given in exchange for the funding. Grants are found on the federal, state and local levels.

Incubator: An incubator is a business development program that usually involves work space, mentoring and business development resources. As opposed to an accelerator, there is usually no timeframe involved in working in an incubator and firms come in and out rather than function as a cohort.

International Economic Development Council (IEDC): A nonprofit membership organization serving economic developers.

Loans (Debt): The amount of money borrowed by one party from another. Companies in the startup and growth stages frequently acquire debt (borrow money) to fuel their startup or growth costs. Debt must be repaid and does not provide any company ownership for the lender.

Makerspace: Makerspaces are places in which people with shared interests, especially in computing or technology, can gather to work on projects while sharing ideas, equipment and knowledge.

Microloan: A very small, short-term loan at low interest, usually to a startup company or self-employed person. The Small Business Administration sponsors a program through which communities can get access to capital for microloan pools.

Minority Business Development Agency (MBDA): Part of the U.S. Department of Commerce, designed to support minority businesses.

Procurement Technical Assistance Center (PTAC): Provides local, in-person training and counseling to help small businesses access federal, state and local contracts. Sponsored in part by the Defense Logistics Agency.

Quadrants of Entrepreneurs: Innovation-Led, Second Stage, Main Street and Microenterprises. See Chapter 2 for definitions.

SCORE: Offers free, confidential business education and mentoring. More than 13,000 volunteer business mentors in chapters across the country; supported by the Small Business Administration.

Seed Investments: Help take a company from proof of concept to market, build a user base and begin scaling. Investment ranges from $250,000 to $1 million.

Service Provider: Any government agency, nonprofit or higher educational program with a specific service or broad-based program to help start or grow small businesses. Also called Resource Partners, Entrepreneurial Support Organizations (ESOs).

Small Business Administration (SBA): A U.S. government agency that provides loan guarantees to make financing available to small businesses. Also supports mentoring, counseling and training.

Small Business Development Center/Small Business and Technology Development Center: Offer free business consulting and low-cost training services. Located throughout the United States; sponsored in part by the Small Business Administration.

Small Business Innovation Research/Small Business Technology Transfer (SBIR/STTR): Federal grant programs that encourage small businesses to engage in research and development that can lead to commercialization. Also provides competitive grants.

SSTI: National organization that supports prosperity through science, technology, innovation and entrepreneurship.

Tech Transfer: Technology transfer is the process of transferring scientific findings from one organization to another for the purpose of further development and commercialization. The process typically includes:

- Identifying new technologies
- Protecting technologies through patents and copyrights
- Providing development and commercialization strategies such as marketing and licensing to existing private sector companies or creating new startup companies based on the technology

University Economic Development Association (UEDA): A membership organization that brings together public and private higher education, private sector, public agencies and community economic development stakeholders.

Venture Capital Firms: Comprise "general partners" who invest funds provided by other "limited partner" investors. Examples of limited partners include pension funds, insurance companies, foundations and ultra high-net-worth individuals. Venture capitalists generally make larger investments than angels, usually from $1 million to $10 million.

Women's Business Centers (WBC): A national network of nearly 100 educational centers that assist women in starting and growing small businesses. Sponsored in part by the Small Business Administration.

11. CLOSING

Looking back, it turns out this was a story of pioneers. It's a story of people working on the front lines of entrepreneurial development, some for more than 25 years. People like Dr. Patricia Greene and Peter deSilva and Don Macke and Norris Krueger and Penny Lewandowski and Steve Radley and Dell Gines and on and on.

And it's proof positive that you can do something to create your entrepreneurial infrastructure, and support your entrepreneurs. You just have to begin.

None of this happens overnight. It takes years … look at all the thriving entrepreneurial communities … they have old and deep roots. And when you're in the middle of it, you may not see the progress. That's why measuring what you can helps keep people from getting discouraged or thinking that it's done.

Not all of it works. It will get messy and there will be failures. Chances are, by the time you read this book, some of the examples we've given will have already closed their doors. But they probably left behind something upon which others can build.

The most fun part of this book has been hearing the stories from people across the country. We know we've just scratched the surface on the subject of what's going on in entrepreneurial communities. We'd love to hear your stories: email us at stories@joinsourcelink.com.

"All of the money in the world cannot solve problems, unless we work together. And if we work together, there is no problem in the world that can stop us, as we seek to develop people to their highest potential."

-Ewing Marion Kauffman

Made in the USA
Lexington, KY
29 April 2019